EXCEPTIONAL CUSTOMER EXPERIENCE

ONE-OF-A-KIND EXPERIENCE THROUGH CUSTOMER SERVICE AND CUSTOMER VALUE BY OPTIMIZING THE CUSTOMER JOURNEY TO ACHIEVE CUSTOMER SUCCESS

JOE LEITOLA

CONTENTS

INTRODUCTION

When you think of your best customer service experience, what comes to mind?

Maybe it was the barista who knew your name and how you liked your latte. Or that time you called customer service, and the agent took pity on you and went out of their way in order to fix the problem. A great customer experience can change the way customers think about a business. You can also build loyalty.

Customer satisfaction is the key metric for measuring customer satisfaction. Having extraordinary customer satisfaction can create competitive differentiation and promotes your brand image. Not just that, customers are the best judge of what your company offers. However, businesses face a constant struggle to handle customer service issues and deliver an exceptional service experience, as it is arguably better to have satisfied customers than dissatisfied customers.

Businesses lose more than $62 billion a year due to poor customer service. And after a bad experience, 51% of customers will never do business with that company again. Therefore, identifying customer service issues and resolving them proactively is critical to building long-term customer relationships and increasing customer loyalty.

Customer service can either make or break a business franchise. However, not everyone agrees on what it is or how to do it right. There are times when customer service work can be challenging. Dealing with different people and trying to meet their expectations is not an easy task.

It takes patience, a keen intellect, and I would even say wisdom to navigate through the various moods of customers and still provide a professional service. This book outlines how to go the extra mile. It shows how important it is to investigate the unseen toxins that damage the customer experience and provides advice on how to improve it. Find out how to stay relevant and thrive in today's business marketplace.

Being a friendly, polite, and empathetic customer service agent is something we always look forward to, and while these are traits that sadly don't always come by default, they are truly an advantage in any customer service situation. In this book, I'll share how to set up your business for customer service success.

This book was created with the intention of helping you understand modern consumers, the modern approach to serving them, and resolving any problems and complaints that arise. The first lesson this book teaches the reader is that awareness is marketing, good product positioning, and first contact with a customer's problem or need. In it, you will find some important tricks that will help you deal with today's buyers. Such as:

- Marketing, what is it, and why is it important?
- How to make sure your option has quality and not fall into the trap of your marketing not matching your services

- What suits your audience? Why is it important to map the type of image you have chosen to give to the platform, for example, Tictok versus linked-in
- What are the different aspects that influence the consideration of the client?
- How selling is consideration persuasion: and how important selling with quality, sustainability and innovation is.
- Sustainability of selling, what is the key element of sustainable selling so you don't sell with bad quality and lose customers in the long run.
- What makes up your mind (psychology behind mind making)
- Make the delivery suit your product or service. How do you choose the right delivery type for your product, and why does this matter
- Why customers are always right (Idea behind this and why it doesn't always be true, but the mindset behind the idea is valid.
- And lost more!

Under pressure for quick results and facing stiff competition in the marketplace, too many marketers find themselves boxed into forms of digital marketing that limit the potential of their long hours, countless experiments, and data warehouses.

And in the end, they see their competition ahead. But what if you build a business around long-term customer relationships, using data to understand who they are, what they need, and where to find more customers like them? You can.

I offer a solution to this goal by asking two simple questions: Why should I be chosen? What makes customers decide? By finding the answers, businesses will be well on their way to success. The book comes with great tools and examples so you can tap into the psyche of today's customers.

Creating an Exceptional Customer Experience authored by myself, a customer service leader with over 5 years of customer service experience, offers several practical strategies to improve customer happiness and loyalty, including cultivating partnerships with customers, providing exclusive membership rewards, and building communities with customers.

I break down the customer journey mapping process and provide insights into exciting and dynamic ways to identify and offer solutions to the challenges they face.

Being a marketing mogul and author, I regularly speak about the importance of 1:1 communication in marketing, and my philosophies extend to the world of customer service as well. I ask readers to build their customer service organization around digital channels, where most customers share their rave reviews as well as their complaints. In the book, I teach readers how to measure customer service productivity, the impact of not responding to customer complaints, and how to use your facility to respond to customer complaints through a variety of channels online.

This book outlines the principles that make for a great customer experience, from the goal of satisfying higher objectives to the importance of putting customers in control. Watkinson fuses human psychology with business strategy for a holistic approach to customer experience (CX) rich in actionable insights based on examples. I encourage companies to identify what their customers value most, prioritize excellence in that business function, as well as accept that this prioritization will result in lower performance in other areas. They argue that customer service will become a competitive differentiator for customers looking to choose from many different options, so this hard truth is also needed.

Every company faces problems when it comes to offering customer service, but what is crucial is the efficiency with which all efforts are being made to solve them.

Solving customer service challenges is a crucial part of running a business as it creates an impact across other lines of business. Excellent customer service creates very loyal customers for life who are willing to recommend your business to friends, family, and colleagues. Providing this kind of great customer service starts with a genuine desire to delight your customers, but you also have to think beyond just selling your products or services. You need to consider the cumulative experience your customers have when they visit your store or website, what they think and feel, and what you can do to improve it.

This book is aimed at customer service leaders to total beginners. It serves as a reminder that the core of customer satisfaction is keeping basic promises and solving daily customer problems. Most clients need not be surprised; they just want products and services to work as promised. Make the customer experience a simple experience to reduce churn, improve customer service, and reduce cost overruns.

1

MAKING SURE YOU ARE NOTICED

Why do all your marketing efforts have to be based on customer awareness? To make people aware of your brand or product and what you have to offer, you need to make people trust you and help them make a decision. This helps you get more sales faster. Is this something you really know? Do you know how this term is used and how a brand is associated with the term? Because this is important, too. Customer service experience is a discipline that puts all customer interactions into one channel so that they work better together. This includes customer expectations, perceptions, and needs that are met or not met.

Customers use the customer experience to talk about how much they want their product, service, or issue to be fixed and how long it will take to get it done. It is important for people to be heard and to be treated fairly. They also want to know that someone will act quickly to solve their problem. The customer doesn't have as much time to look over information and wants a supplier who can give strong support and advice, as well as deal with problems quickly. I don't need to tell you that making people more aware is a hard job. It's also true that 89 percent of marketers say that getting people to know about their brand is their main goal (West, C. 2021). A successful, well-known brand is instantly recognizable, loved, and even revered by its customers, and sometimes even the whole world, too. These are some of the things that customer awareness strategies can help you do with your brand or product, in general.

WHAT IS CUSTOMER AWARENESS?

When a buyer has a good understanding of a product or company, they can get the most out of their purchases. A lot of good decisions can be made by consumers when they have information about what to buy and how much to pay for things, like cars. Consumers will be better off if they know their rights and read alerts and warnings.

At the top of the marketing funnel, people become aware. The more we know about customers, the more empathy we have for each one. Is it a common goal or theme in your company to rise to the top of your field? It all starts with customers getting to know your brand.

The Coca-Cola brand has to be the best at making people aware of their products. 94 percent of the world's people know their logo (Basin. K. 2011). It doesn't matter if you don't like fizzy drinks, because this is a very good thing to do. Coca-Cola never lets a chance to show you their branding pass them by, even if you don't know it's them. They don't just want to be famous to show off. It's an effective, well-thought-out strategy to make people aware of their brand. They'll be known to everyone who's born. When they're thirsty, they'll reach for the drink they've seen everyone else drinking. It's how people feel when they know about a brand.

For any coach or business that wants to connect with their customers, a blanket marketing strategy isn't going to work. It's important that your marketing strategy fits the continuum of people who buy from you. Potential customers range from people who have never heard of you to people who already know and trust you.

WHAT IS MARKETING?

Let's face it: to most business people, marketing is just promotion, and that's what it means. Marketing is what you say and how you say it when you want to show people how great your product is and why they should buy. It's like an ad. It's like having a brochure. An important part of marketing is putting out a press release. There are now Facebook pages and Twitter accounts that people use to market their business. Many business people think that marketing is just selling on a bigger scale.

We can say that marketing is finding out what people want and need and then providing goods and services that meet or exceed those needs and wants. This is what marketing is all about. Marketing is about making deals. It is called an exchange when two people give each other something of value in order to meet their own needs or wants. The truth is that marketing is at the intersection of the business and the customer. It is the great judge between the business's needs and the needs of the customer.

WHY MARKETING IS IMPORTANT?

You can advertise your product, but you can also do consumer research, which helps you better match your product to what people want and need. This is also a form of marketing, because it helps your company's products and services match up with known customer needs. Marketing is like the heart of your business, and it needs to be done well. The more you put out there about your business, the more healthy it will be. For your business to stay alive, you need to do more marketing.

Your business could have ground-breaking, industry-changing products and services that meet your customers' needs but not have a chance to reach your target audience if you don't market them. Your company's sales may not meet your goals, and it will be more difficult for you to grow your business.

1) Makes people more aware:

Most of the time, we see an ad or get a recommendation, but we don't always buy or use the product or service right away. By marketing, you will build a group of people who know who you are, what you can do, and where to find you when they are ready to buy your products or services.

2) Increases sales:

The more people know about the product, the more sales there will be for new people and for the company that sells a unique product in the market. A good marketing campaign can help the sales of a business go up. Sales go up, which means that the business makes more money. This money is put back into the business to make more money in the future. It is very important for a new business to be good at marketing in order for it to last. Today, the value of marketing is very high in business.

3) Establishes trust between your business and your customers:

To make your small business as successful as possible, you need to build a group of people who love your brand. To buy products and/or services from you, people are going to have to keep coming back to your business. To do this, you need to build up a certain level of trust with your clients. He or she needs to be able to trust you to give them the best goods and/or services at the best prices. Marketing helps to build some trust between businesses and their clients. The way companies market their products and services can help them build trust with their customers and keep them coming back for more products and services in the future, too.

4) People want to buy from a business that has a good reputation:

They want to know that they can trust the business they are going to buy something from. It takes a long time to build trust and a good name for your business. When your business can build trust with your customers, it makes them more likely to stay with you. If your clients are happy with your products or services, they will talk about your business. Word of mouth is the most effective type of marketing, and it's free.

5) Source of new ideas:

Marketing helps businesses to understand the need of customers reviews from customers serves in the improvement of the current products. There is a rapid evolution in the tastes and choices of people. Marketing helps in getting these changes. It helps to understand new demand models that appeared in the market. This is how the analysis and improvement department improves things.

· · ·

6) Teaches you about your business' customer base:

When you start a small business, you might have a general idea of who your customers will be based on the products and services you have to offer. It might be that over time, you find that your target audience isn't who you thought it would be.

Market research can teach you a lot about your customer base. You can look at who responds the best to your marketing efforts and use that information to change up who you are marketing to.

7) Tackling the competition:

It's getting more and more competitive in almost every part of the economy. The trust that people have in any business is hard to build. There are many things that marketing can do to help people think of your brand as a "icon." Marketing not only helps to get the product and service to the customers, but it also makes them want to buy it. People who know how to market their business better than their competitors can use new technology to make their business more powerful. People who use marketing to get ahead of their business rivals can beat them. It is easier to get the whole market if you use productive marketing.

STAGES OF CUSTOMER AWARENESS

All businesses have trouble getting customer awareness of their brand. Some businesses have a hard time getting customers to know about both their brand and the customer's problem. Some businesses are in a particularly difficult situation because they have to make sure customers know about both their brand and the customer's problem at the same time. Some people don't even know they need you yet. When your product or service is very new, this can happen. You have to start over with a customer who has a problem but doesn't know how to solve it. Some people don't even know they need you yet. When your product or service is very new, this can happen. You have to start over with a customer who has a problem but doesn't know how to solve it.

In Breakthrough Advertising (<u>Schwartz 2004</u>), Schwartz said that "customer awareness" is very important. Better still, he made it all the same. Schwartz came up with five different types of customer awareness marketing campaign-strategy. Since then, many marketers have done the same thing.

1) Most aware customers:

Your service or product will help this customer, but they don't know how much it costs or how long it will last. He or she already knows what you do. The person who is the most aware has already been taught. They want to know how much things cost. This customer wants to see what you have to offer, what comes with it, and how much it costs.

The Most Aware customer knows so much about your service or product that you need strong iconic branding and emotional marketing to make your business or product stand out from the crowd. You have to work harder to make your product or service stand out if your customers are "most aware."

2) Product aware:

It's at this point in the process that the prospect has an idea of what they want, but they don't know how to get it (they know about your competitor's products). It's just that they don't know much about your product or brand.

They don't know if what you offer is right for them. They don't want just any information. They want to know if your product or service meets their needs. You need to beat the competition. Tell the customer why you are better than other options, brands, and alternatives. It's important for your marketing and sales to know exactly how your competition isn't as good as you are, so they can crush them.

It's time to fill them all in. Sell the benefits of using your product/services to this particular prospect. Present them with case studies, reports, analysis and testimonials. The key is to deliver real content with the benefit of your offer demonstrated. Of course, always include a well-crafted landing page at the end.

3) Solution aware customers:

Solution Aware Customers know the results they want but they don't know how your product will deliver. They need to know how you meet their need. They intimately understand and live their need, they know the outcome / solution they want. What they need to know is, how do you solve their need?

Set an outcome or potential future state for this customer, a goal they want to achieve. This customer is probably hearing a lot of competing claims about benefits and it's all sounding like noise. You need product features, or service features, to differentiate yourself, and back these up with facts. It's not about making bold claims but focusing on your features and data, information and third party validation. Marketing to these customers involves creating a potential future state or outcome for this person, a goal they want to achieve

4) Problem aware:

This stage is for customers who are aware that they have a problem but may not completely understand it or what solutions are out there. These people have no idea what you do, how you do it, or what other businesses like yours do. Because they know they have a problem, but can't figure out how to fix it, a problem-aware customer is the most annoyed by this

This is when you figure out who your target market is and what they're going through. Find out what keywords people search for when they search for things like content marketing, blogging, videos, and so on. Content that has its own value is important for anyone who came to your page through a search engine or a social media site, because they need to see strong content. Make sure your content tells them about their problems and suggests possible solutions. After that, he asks them to sign up for more news. Focus on building trust with them before you try to get them to sign up for something. Make sure that your content is search engine optimized. This would be a great chance to show them what your company is all about.

5) Unaware customers:

They don't even know they have a problem, need or desire. Some people may not feel the "pain" we see. There are still a lot of things that they believe about the world and how things work. They may be resistant to solutions to problems that aren't well-targeted. This is a hard group to market to because it takes a long time and a lot of work to get them to buy. Thus, it's the most expensive way to market to them because they are the most likely to buy. The customer may not be interested in a "solution" that isn't well-placed. Marketers who are less strategic will focus on people who can help them get customers, like referring professionals or family caregivers. When they start talking to the actual customer, they'll get a lot of resistance from them.

The way you can connect with these customers is to talk to them about how they feel. Find out what their goal or motivation is, and grow a desire from that goal. They will need more information, more visual stories, and more testimonies in order to become more aware.

HOW DO YOU RAISE QUALITY AWARENESS?

Do you ask for a coke or a cola when getting a drink at a fast-food restaurant? What about when you self-injure? Are you looking for a plastic bandage or a Band-Aid?

These names are referred to as proprietary eponyms, and they represent the pinnacle of product awareness. These trademarks have grown so well-known in our language that they have supplanted generic words for similar things. To get proprietary eponym status for a product is essentially the ultimate of product recognition. While you may not be able to accomplish this with your small business, that does not mean you cannot do much more to increase brand awareness.

Improving product quality is critical for long-term profitability and growth in sales. While improving product quality is not a simple endeavor, the advantages far outweigh the difficulties. It contributes to the development of trust with your consumer and encourages recommendations and referrals. Additionally, superior product quality results in fewer customer complaints and returns. These mentioned factors have an effect on your bottom line and help your business flourish. So how can you increase consumer awareness of your items' quality?

1) Define quality through the eyes of your consumer:

Knowing precisely what your consumers desire is critical for quality improvement. Define what areas require improvement in light of the experience and impressions you want your consumers to have of your services and goods. Put yourself in their place and attempt to think through their eyes. What aspect of your product or service would they adore? Is it the fit, aesthetics, speed, efficiency, safety, or warranty? Enumerate what is most important to them and establish specific goals for improvement in that area. When it comes to always staying ahead of the competition in today's world, understanding the element is just as critical as developing measures to improve the quality.

2) Appearance:

It is said that one should not judge a book just by its cover. However, isn't that what everyone does? There is little we can actually do about it; this has always been the case; the initial impression is critical. Once a poor first impression is created, it is virtually hard to reverse it. This is true even in our everyday lives; job interviews, first dates, and, yes, product interactions.

At the end of the day, it is what forms people's perceptions of a product and influences their decision to continue using it or not.

3) Invest in machinery:

If the majority of your manufacturing is done by hand, your products are more prone to mistakes and flaws. Having stated that, you must invest in high-quality machinery. Precision manufacturing machinery promotes constant product quality. Additionally, machines aid in increasing production speed and

are far less expensive than hiring multiple experienced
employees.

4) Monitor your rivals:

Monitoring your competitors helps you grow and enhance
the quality of your items. Competitor analysis enables you to
identify the advantages and disadvantages of your rivals' goods
in relation to your own and to identify market gaps.

How effective are their products? Examine their goods for
flaws and attempt to provide an inventive solution for yours.
Additionally, you might receive new ideas that you can develop
to make your product more desirable and appeal to clients.
Conducting a competition analysis is critical not just for
matching your rivals' products but also for positioning you to
compete against comparable firms in your sector.

5) Consider comments and respond appropriately:

Maintaining a constant, high-quality connection with your
consumers is also one of the most effective approaches to
improving the product's quality. Establish a line of contact with
your customers by soliciting regular feedback and adjusting
your sales presentation, advertising campaigns, production
techniques, and day-to-day operations to better serve them. It
is paramount to maintain a strong relationship with your
established client base in the modern age of digital communications. You can always rely on their feedback on your products,
designs, or services. Because customers hold the keys to
increasing sales, interacting with them will go a long way
toward providing high-quality products and services.

POPULAR PLATFORMS AND TOOLS USED TO RAISE QUALITY AWARENESS

By increasing brand awareness, you enhance your chances of generating leads — and perhaps sales. While raising awareness may seem challenging, it does not have to be. A successful, established brand is instantly known, beloved, and appreciated by its consumers and occasionally the entire globe. When your brand is recognized, it becomes simpler to increase brand awareness, which indicates how well-known your product is as well as how familiar your target audience is with its traits and attributes.

Continue reading to discover prominent platforms/tools that can assist you in achieving your product awareness objectives.

1) Newspaper advertising:

The habit of reading newspapers is widespread among educated people. Apart from daily newspapers, there are also biweekly and weekly publications. Newspapers are distributed worldwide and are read by a diverse range of individuals.

As a result, newspapers may be a very effective tool for raising quality awareness. When choosing a newspaper, for this reason, an advertiser must evaluate the newspaper's circulation, the demographic of its readers, the geographic location in which it is popular, and the cost of space.

2) Social media:

According to a 2020 research by Datareportal (Simon Kemp, 2020), We Are Social, and Hootsuite, social media users usually spend an average of two hours and twenty-four minutes each day across an average of eight social networks and messaging applications. Facebook continues to be the most popular of these networks, followed by YouTube and Instagram.

Social media has revolutionized the means businesses interact with their consumers online. You may utilize social media to attract new clients and maintain contact with current ones. Small businesses may now obtain the type of visibility once reserved for large companies with large expenditures. Several social media networks are worth noting:

- **Twitter:**

Twitter enables public dialogue in real-time. You can post brief comments as well as links to online pages, blogs, and photos. This enables individuals to comment openly, therefore fostering dialogue. By including links, you may increase the number of visitors to your website. Additionally, you may retweet posts that catch your eye. Twitter enables you to amass a network of followers and, in turn, to follow those with whom you wish to connect. It's an opportunity to showcase your greatest qualities by sharing expertise, replying to comments and inquiries, and developing partnerships.

- **Facebook:**

By posting news and material and being kind and helpful on Facebook, you can demonstrate the human side of your organization. Encourage your audience to contribute material and offer comments, and respond immediately to complaints. Facebook provides both analytical tools and advertising options.

- **Instagram:**

Instagram is a popular social media platform chaired by Facebook that enables users to upload photos and short video snippets. With the help of filters and other tools, you may enhance your recordings and photographs. Hashtags enable you to spread the word about your work. Encourage people to share their own videos and photographs about your company.

- **LinkedIn:**

LinkedIn is the business-to-business networking software for professionals, consultants, and businesses. You may create a personal or business profile and invite colleagues, friends, and even rivals to join your network. Take caution not to oversell; LinkedIn is a platform for sharing material and assisting others in raising their profile. Solicit endorsements and testimonials from acquaintances and reciprocate.

- **Pinterest:**

Pinterest is a visual social media medium that is great for retail and lifestyle businesses looking to increase referrals and sales. You "pin" photos to boards and urge your followers to do the same. Rich Pins enable you to show product information, such as pricing and shipping information, as well as connections to your website. Encourage individuals to re-pin your photographs and your own to increase your profile.

3) Word of mouth:

Word of mouth marketing (affectionately dubbed WOMM) has the power to build or ruin a firm. It has the ability to both construct and destroy. If you operate a small business, word of mouth may be the nicest thing since sliced bread — or it might seem like doling out doses of hemlock to prospective clients. Which metaphor is appropriate relies on the type of word of mouth around your business?

In our technologically advanced culture, word of mouth is more critical than ever. Online reviews are accessible for everything from surgeons to dog walkers, and research by Bright-Local found that nearly 9 in 10 customers get information online, evaluations of local companies, and 72% indicated they utilized favorable ratings to establish a business's trustworthiness (Bright Ideas, 2022).

Word of mouth marketing is not a fast answer for your issues; it is a long journey with a large payout if you are willing to make the road. Begin your extraordinary adventure with the following five steps, and then continue walking:

- **Step 1: Give your audience a reason to rave:**

Word of mouth marketing is most effective for companies who are committed to doing the right thing for their consumers. This entails a strong offering complemented by superb customer service. Obviously, your product must be strong, but as crucial is the personnel that interacts with consumers and clients.

- **Step 2: Be individualistic:**
- One strategy for generating word of mouth is to make your business genuinely remarkable. This can be accomplished in a variety of ways, including the following:
- a one-of-a-kind item
- unmatched corporate culture

- innovative marketing strategies

- **Step 3: Establish yourself as an industry thought leader:**

Do you want people to talk about you? Prove yourself as a thoughtful leader in your field! This will demand significant work on your part — you'll need to engage in discussion with established business leaders and power players while also remaining current on industry news. Once you've gained sufficient knowledge and confidence, you may create your own forecasts and conclusions based on industry patterns. Simply ensure that you can substantiate your hypotheses with empirical proof.

- **Step 4: Establish a positive reputation for yourself:**

There will be no sleazy methods used here. Develop your reputation by being respectful to and serving your consumers fairly. Avoid attempting to swindle your consumers, and they will reward you profusely.

- **Step 5: An active, engaged social community:**

A close-knit social community may also help generate word-of-mouth marketing. Online communities can be formed in the following ways: through fostering discourse.

- hosting competitions
- coordinating events (online and offline)
- programs of loyalty

The most effective word-of-mouth marketing campaign persuades consumers that by purchasing their goods, they are making a personal statement and entering exclusive ranks. As particular products or services become ingrained in a customer's identity, die-hard enthusiasts may even refer to beloved companies as "family."

3) Email marketing:

Email marketing and email campaigns give businesses several options to communicate with their subscribers and keep them informed about the brand's activities.

Email marketing is the practice of sending commercial emails to a list of contacts who have given you express permission to interact with them via email. Through the usage of a newsletter, you can leverage email marketing to update your contacts, increase sales, as well as establish a community around your business.

Modern email marketing has shifted away from bulk mailings that are one-size-fits-all and toward permission, segmentation, and personalization. While this may look like a time a time-consuming process, marketing automation takes care of the heavy lifting for you.

4) Branding:

Branding is the ongoing process of discovering, developing, and managing the cumulative assets and behaviors that influence how stakeholders perceive a brand.

Branding is critical since it not only creates a lasting impression on consumers but also informs them about what to anticipate from your business. It's a technique of differentiating yourself from the competition and emphasizing what makes you the superior pick. Your brand is developed to accurately reflect who you are as a business and how you intend to be viewed.

5) Improve your website's search engine optimization:

Search engine optimization (SEO) allows your website to rank higher in Google's search results. By including relevant keywords throughout your business's web pages and blog posts, you may boost the likelihood that consumers will find your site while conducting an internet search for businesses similar to yours. However, SEO entails much more than keyword usage, and it's beneficial to conduct some study online or locate a book that details how to optimize your site's search engine performance. Additionally, you may wish to consider employing an SEO service to assist with website optimization.

6) Paid advertising:

Paid advertising may be an effective strategy to drive more visitors to your website and grow your business, but it can be a costly undertaking if you are inexperienced. As the term indicates, paid to advertise is internet advertising that is purchased. Pay-Per-Click (PPC), programmatic advertising, Google Ads, Google Display, Facebook Ads, Twitter Ads, LinkedIn Ads, and Google and Facebook retargeting are all examples of paid advertising.

Paid advertisements are then served to an audience defined by the advertiser in the ad platform. And, as the name refers, you only pay when someone clicks on your advertisement. Along with paying per click, some marketers arrange their advertising to pay per 1000 views (CPM), otherwise known as impressions. To learn more about sponsored advertising, read this article from **(Innovation visual).**

HOW TO CHOOSE THE RIGHT PLATFORM?

There is no longer any iota of doubt that social media is an indispensable marketing tool for any organization seeking to maintain relevance and visibility. This implies that if you're not maximizing your use of social media, you're passing up a significant opportunity. However, getting started may be challenging, and even something as relatively straightforward as selecting a social media site might be more involved than you believe. There are several social media platforms available, and selecting your channels and developing a plan might be difficult.

When it comes to determining the ideal social media strategy for your business, the first step is to establish a priority list. Is it broadening your horizons? Is it increasing lead generation? Is it a matter of brand recognition? Following that, it's a matter of selecting which platform will provide you with the most exposure to the most relevant audience. Is your brand very visual, making it well-suited for sites such as Instagram or TikTok? Is it time-sensitive, and will it function well on Twitter? Or is your audience diversified, necessitating the use of many channels, such as YouTube and LinkedIn?

The guidelines outlined below will help you in selecting your platform and making the best options possible based on the most critical aspects.

·   ·   ·

1) What is the nature of your business?

To begin, determine the kind of your business. To conduct a thorough analysis, respond to a few questions that provide a comprehensive picture of your organization.

- What sort of business do you operate?
- Is it regional or global in scope?
- Is your firm an internet retailer?
- Who is your intended audience (gender, age)?

Each product has an audience, and each audience has its own advertising platform that enables you to connect with that set of individuals. Your task is to match your business requirements to the capabilities of the platform.

2) How does your target audience communicate?

You must evaluate the platforms on which your audience interacts online. Having an Instagram account for your company, for example, may be a waste of time if your primary target demographic is 70-year-old women. Similarly, there may be no compelling reason to promote your business on Pinterest if your target audience is exclusively male.

Social media demographics inform the most focused and effective social media strategy. These data-driven insights will guarantee that your strategy and channel selection provide the most relevant, tailored approach possible, increasing your conversion rate.

Utilizing a social listening tool enables you to do an analysis of your present followers. This will offer you gender, age, and geographical information on your present social audiences, allowing you to choose which channels are worth sustaining and which are not.

. . .

3) What is your advertising campaign's objective?

When it comes to advertising platforms, the primary consideration should be your advertising objective.

Consider the following:

- Do you wish to present your brand to the world?
- Do you want to raise brand recognition, or do you already have a strong brand and want to send visitors to your product pages in order to improve sales? Define your objective.

Your advertising platform is determined by your objectives. If your target audience is new to your brand and unfamiliar with it, you are in the awareness stage. You must proceed cautiously. You may create a video that showcases your product and all of its features.

If your business is well-established and you're interested in marketing to your fans on social media, you've reached the buying stage. You may provide discounts and special promotions to help you advertise your business.

4) What type of material are you looking to produce?

This is a critical point since there are several content kinds — some of which will compliment your company objectives and brand identity, while others will not. Additionally, certain types of information will be better suited to specific social platforms than others.

5) Which channels do your rivals use?

As critical as researching the networks your target audience uses in determining which social media platforms your rivals utilize. This establishes a benchmark against which you may measure industry activity and informs your actions.

Consider the sort of material they publish. Do they generate material that is platform-specific? How frequently are they posting it? How many likes or shares do they receive on their posts? Examining your rivals' social media activity, as well as how successfully their followers connect with their content, can give you vital information that you can emulate to ensure your strategy's success.

HOW DO THE ACTIONS AND OBJECTIVES OF YOUR CUSTOMERS INTERSECT WITH YOUR APPROACH TO AWARENESS?

Understanding the fundamental functions of product awareness will assist you in focusing your efforts and plans to support your business more effectively. Additionally, it's much easier to demonstrate ROI and relevant KPIs when you understand exactly what the marketing department is supposed to produce. However, with the advent of the Internet and social media, consumer behavior has shifted tremendously. Not only has social media become a necessary component of every marketing plan, but buyers now want relationships with businesses that extend beyond the use of their goods.

A small but rising number of providers in business marketplaces leverage their understanding of what consumers value and would appreciate in order to obtain a competitive edge over less-informed competitors. These suppliers have created customer value models, which are data-driven representations of the monetary value of the work they are doing or could do for their clients. Customer value models are constructed using cost-benefit analyses of a particular market offering in a particular customer application. Depending on the conditions, such as the availability of data and the participation of a customer, a supplier may develop a value model for an individual client or a market sector, using data acquired from several consumers in that segment.

Customer behavior analysis is critical for marketers because it enables them to comprehend consumer expectations. It's beneficial to understand why a buyer purchases a product. It is critical to determine the types of items that people want before releasing them to the market. Marketers may ascertain consumer preferences and build marketing campaigns accordingly. Consumer activity studies examine a variety of topics, including what customers purchase, why they buy, when they buy, why they buy, and how frequently they buy.

2

WHY SHOULD YOU BE CHOSEN

Competition between businesses can be fierce, especially in rapidly changing markets where customers often shop around. If you're an entrepreneur, you've no doubt heard the statistics on business failure rates. Only 50% of the companies are more than five years old, and a third are more than ten years old (<u>Dean & Beer, 2022</u>)

Regardless of the industry a company operates in, even if it is relatively new or small, careful research will reveal two or more competitors. His existence immediately changes the playing field. In a concentrated effort to take that step forward, companies adopt numerous competitive strategies to increase their competitive advantage.

SELLING

How do you get your customers to buy what you sell? When your products and brand are new to the market, you'll find yourself asking this question. Your profitability and the life of your business depend on the sales generated by your customers. Therefore, you may have to go to great lengths to persuade them to consume your goods or services. Enhancing your product quality is one of the most necessary things to achieve long-term sales growth and profitability. While enhancing product quality is no easy task, it does reward companies with higher revenues and lower costs.

You need to make it very clear to potential attendees that you are the only option for them. How do you go from being one of the many fish in the sea to being the fish that everyone wants? This can be a difficult task, but not impossible, using these few tips on how to stand out from the competition and thus get more attendees.

1) Tell the truth

If you are producing quality products and offering excellent services, there is no need to lie and exaggerate just to attract buyers. The only thing you need is, to tell the truth about your products. With light and truth in your hands, you can encourage customers to ask questions and respond with confidence. The trust you have in your words will also trust your customers, who will ultimately trust you and buy your products.

2) Use the power of social proof

Consumers' lack of trust in advertisements is not news. Indeed, research continually demonstrates that customers would rather trust an online stranger than a business attempting to sell them anything. With social proof, you can leverage this to your advantage.

Simply put, social proof is the process of using the activities of current customers to persuade prospective customers to buy.

The most frequently used method is testimonials. Simply collect testimonials from your customers and place them in prominent locations on your website, landing pages, and product pages.

3) Develop a strong understanding of your client

By developing a strong understanding of your client, you can define everything from the tone of voice you'll use in your sales presentation to the modes of communication you'll use to reach out to potential buyers. Create a Buyer Persona to accomplish this. Recognize who your ideal client is and conduct extensive research to ascertain what would sway him and what might turn him off.

In this manner, you may avoid using strategies that will alienate potential buyers and instead focus on the strongest arguments that will persuade them that your product is the solution they've been searching for.

4) Identify and leverage your USP

USP also stands for Unique Selling Point, and it is essentially about emphasizing the distinct advantages you offer in order to differentiate yourself from the competitors. Why would someone choose your firm over another delivering the same or a comparable service? What specific advantages do you have that your competitors lack? The more difficult it is to copy your unique selling proposition, the larger your competitive edge.

Is it challenging for you to communicate your unique selling proposition? Inquire about your former clients! Why did they pick you specifically? What were they most pleased with as a

result of their patronage of your business? This might help you
determine what makes your firm special.

5) Establish a long-term relationship

People are dubious in the short and long term. Even if you
have a decent product, it is not guaranteed to be perfect. We all
face reality and make errors. However, individuals or customers
are seeking more than a great product; they are looking for
responsible sellers, manufacturers, or businesses that will
always be available to assist them and answer to their demands
at any time. Buyers want to be completely satisfied with their
purchase. If you want them to purchase your items, you must
demonstrate to them that they will not regret doing business
with you by maintaining contact and developing a positive,
long-lasting, shining relationship with them.

6) Avoid imposing your perspective

It may seem counterintuitive to imply that you should
refrain from offering your opinion when attempting to convince
someone to purchase something. The point is that you can say
whatever you believe is best for your prospective buyer, but you
must do so in an unimpressive manner. Make your arguments
as subtle as possible and demonstrate that your perspective
matters.

UNDERSTANDING CUSTOMER VALUE

Customer value is critical to the acquisition, development, and
retention of customers. Businesses would be irresponsible if
they did not seek to enhance it and sustain profitable client
connections. Contrary to its name, it does not refer to the

value-added by a customer to a business, which is not to say that customers do not contribute value. Rather than that, customer value refers to the level of satisfaction a customer experiences or anticipates as a result of taking action in relation to the cost of that activity. Businesses must give this value, as over 66% of customers worldwide believe it is critical for businesses to understand their individual wants and expectations (Nextiva 2021). When a business serves its target market effectively, its members benefit from increased customer value.

Adding value to customers improves their satisfaction and experience. A positive customer experience adds value to a customer. Creating customer value boosts customer loyalty, market share, and pricing while also reducing errors and increasing efficiency. Increased market share and efficiency result in increased earnings. Consumers frequently evaluate the perceived worth of similar products and services when making purchasing decisions. They then choose the offerings that have the best client lifetime value out of all those on the market. Due to the fact that each customer has their own set of needs, desires, and resources, no two consumers will place the exact value on the same service or product.

HOW TO CREATE CUSTOMER VALUE?

Creating customer value entails providing something of value in exchange for something of greater worth to you. You could produce a high-value product for yourself, but your customers see no reason to. You don't generate sales, which means you're not adding any value to your own life.

Creating value for the consumer takes into consideration a variety of elements. You must audit all of your consumer touchpoints and determine how they may be optimized. These are

only some of the topics deserving investigating for potential
value generation.

1) Conduct an audit of your brand's value proposition

Your brand value proposition differentiates you from the
market's hundreds of commercial competitors. A value proposition explains why your audience should do business with you
and the benefits they can expect.

But, the unfortunate reality is that the most of businesses
fail to convey the appropriate value proposition through their
marketing activities. Rather than that, their efforts are suffo-
cated by useless platitudes and clichés.

2) Consistency

To develop a strong relationship with customers and drive
repeat sales, it is critical to maintaining a consistent level of
product and service quality. If a customer is satisfied with their
initial purchase, they will make more purchases with the expec-
tation that the quality will be maintained. Businesses must
establish benchmarks for themselves. This enables them to
maintain a high standard of quality for their products or
services.

3) Purchase or construct commodities

Frequently, you earn the majority of your revenues prior to
making a sale. In the real estate market, there is a saying that
you earn when you buy a property, not when you sell it. This
indicates that there is a greater likelihood of profiting from
finding homes at a discount than there is of profiting from
selling at a premium.

Many bankers, particularly lenders, believe that loans generate the greatest profit margins for banks. Banks usually acquire most of their revenue from loans. The price of bank shares, on the other hand, is determined by the strength of the bank's deposits rather than its loans. Deposits are more valuable than loans in the market. When you see cash, it's natural to associate it with worth. It's common to conflate revenue-generating businesses with those that create the majority of value. In the banking example above, the loan interest is a source of revenue for the bank, whereas deposit interest paid to depositors is a source of revenue for the depositors. How is it possible that something that generates expenses is more valuable than something that provides revenue?

The trick is to view your organization as a complicated system of value-creating operations. One approach to think about it is to partition the entire system into components and imagine that each process is a self-contained entity.

4) Collect and analyze client feedback

Customers are the finest source of information on what gives value to them. Conduct timely surveys with them to ascertain their priorities. Customers frequently do not mind paying a premium for a superior customer experience. Indeed, they are willing to spend up to 16% extra for a superior customer experience. Therefore, rather than assuming what is more desirable to them, inquire directly and work for it.

5) Provide relevant content to your audience

Your branded content strategy should not be all about you. To add value to your customers, you must generate material that is important to the — content that they truly need, and that will help them grow.

You can educate your clients by sharing how-to manuals, tutorials, or webinars. Additionally, you may publish brand-specific content (product details and features) that instruct users on how to acquire the most out of your service or product. This will assist your brand in cultivating a learning community that participates with your brand in order to obtain the most value from the products you sell.

HOW TO IMPROVE CUSTOMER VALUE OF YOUR BUSINESS?

Customer expectations are a lot higher than they have ever been, and your customers are more scrutinizing than ever. They are comparing their interaction with your business to the straightforward, quick, and personalized interactions they have with the best of the best. And it is these customer-centric businesses that will profit from increased loyalty and competitive advantage.

Calculating customer value provides critical insight into the health of your organization. When customer value is out of balance, it indicates a problem within the firm. A thorough grasp of customer value enables you to strengthen your business's predictability and determine the best course of action for increasing your margin. The following are tried-and-true strategies for increasing average customer value and increasing revenue from existing customers.

1) Determine what motivates client loyalty

The more loyal a customer is, the bigger the customer's value. Therefore, study what motivates loyalty. Numerous businesses focus exclusively on the Net Promoter Score (NPS). A far more compelling question is why a customer would suggest you or not. Inquire about a variety of factors, including brand perception, connection to your firm, product quality, service speed, a sense of added value, communication, and value for money.

2) Provide superior customer service

Investing in superior customer service is an essential component of growing your business and increasing client loyalty. If your service is below average, even if your product is above average, clients will choose your competitors over you tell the truth. According to data, one-third of consumers are likely to switch brands as a result of one episode of poor customer service (Smith 2022).

As such, it is critical to obtain the appropriate customer assistance. A higher level of customer service equates to a higher level of customer experience. As a result, existing clients will be more likely to become long-term, committed customers.

3) Simplify

Choice has become a double-edged sword. Since switching costs have fallen, for example, for gas and electricity, life has become more complicated. Technology breeds worry and discomfort; media messages produce a cacophony that pervades public restrooms; and the variety of twenty jeans styles, 24 jam tastes, and 22 cell phone models is overwhelming. Consumers seek counsel and personal information from trusted sources such as friends, family, networks, and advisors. The lesson for businesses is to innovate rather than copy and to

promote public relations and media relations in conjunction
with advertising.

4) Simplify onboarding

It is very natural for individuals to seek out the least
demanding method of accomplishing a task. Likewise, our
buying experiences are similar. Buyers need simplicity, and
nowhere is this more evident than at the outset of the
purchasing process.

Be it you're a new business owner or an established one, the
following approaches will help you build a flawless buying
experience:

- Maintain an up-to-date, aesthetically pleasing, and
  user-friendly website that is geared for mobile
  devices. Conduct a user test to identify issues. If you
  own a physical store, keep it neat and tidy and use
  signage to indicate the whereabouts of various
  things.
- Tutorial information such as films, how-to articles,
  and webinars can assist potential consumers in
  determining the correct things to order or how to
  use the payment system.
- From the start, keep your focus on the value of your
  business proposition. Allow buyers to make an
  educated assumption about what is healthy for
  them if they make a purchase.
- Using ERP integration and automation to meet the
  growing demands and problems of online shopping
  while lowering costs and saving time is an excellent
  method to do it.

- Make the exit process as simple as possible. Utilizing shopping cart software streamlines and expedites the ordering process.

Accepting as well as processing debit and credit card payments is a must for all online businesses. The correct account provider will assist you in trading efficiently.

Send new customers a welcome email outlining the services they may expect from you in the future.

5) Concentrate your efforts on your most significant consumers

Increased time and resource allocation to the most profitable client segment is another effective technique for increasing customer value. Provide these consumers with a more personalized customer experience, so they feel honored to do business with you. For instance, when you request technical assistance, your support team may already be aware of your details. This saves them time by allowing them to identify themselves using your credentials and strengthens your relationship with them.

KEY ELEMENTS OF SUSTAINABLE SELLING

It is normal for a business to use its complete genetic composition in order to advertise itself and differentiate itself in its market. For example, SMEs frequently leverage bottom-up startups or a local strategy to establish a distinct tone of voice, whereas larger enterprises take satisfaction in winning industry accolades. Another method that businesses can make use of is sustainable selling, which can be used for both product and brand marketing.

Sustainable Sales is not a static state of equilibrium but an evolutionary process in which the allocation of sales resources, the direction of investments, the orientation of technology progress, and institutional change are balanced against future and present needs. It's about redefining and reformulating "growth" and "sales," as well as introducing "sustainable selling" ideas into business training, consulting, and coaching (sales coaching).

Additionally, these tactics assist you in developing the types of long-term partnerships vital to assist your firm in remaining viable and being successful.

1) Identify a greater purpose

The first premise of sustainable marketing is to view your organization in ways other than through the lens of its financial figures. Sustainability begins with deriving a purpose for all of your business's actions and selling that purpose as a free-for-all idea. For instance, if you work in the plastic product manufacturing industry, the first step toward sustainability is to use a particular percentage of recycled plastic in your products. You can then undertake sustainable marketing by pushing others to purchase them: in this way, you are inviting people to help you achieve your goal of strengthening the reuse and recycling mentality in business.

2) Understand your market

Gaining a thorough understanding of your target market, particularly why people buy your products or services, is critical for utilizing the most effective sustainability marketing tactics to capture their attention. Not only will you save time and money by avoiding segments that are uninterested in what you're selling, but you'll also save paper and resources by avoiding sending printed marketing materials to unresponsive prospects. Determine whether your target market responds to direct mail postcards or to email marketing messages that do not require printing, postage, or postage. If you opt-out of direct mail, make sure to emphasize the sustainability benefits of your decision in other marketing.

3) Begin with the products

Sustainable selling requires sustainable product development and production. It is critical to visualize the entire product life cycle in order to incorporate sustainability. Where can you obtain raw materials that are completely harmless? How can operations be optimized to release less carbon into the atmosphere? After the transaction, how do you anticipate your customers will interact with the packaging? Is each stage of a product's life cycle environmentally sustainable? These are the critical questions that must be addressed.

It is a thorough examination of company operations, but it is all for the greater benefit. You can begin by taking little steps as well as using sustainable marketing to raise awareness of your work and keep the community informed.

4) Foster alliances

Not just strategic and business connections but also those at the granular level within an organization must embed sustainability. From supply chain to distributors, department to department, you should be committed to supporting sustainable practices throughout. Your ethics are certain to have an effect on those with whom you associate and propagate.

Sustainable marketing also entails informing consumers about sustainable collaboration projects.

For instance, the fast fashion industry may seek to develop a coalition dedicated to recycling old fabric rather than purchasing new to create clothing that swiftly goes out of style and is discarded.

5) Eliminate inefficient tactics

Pursuing prospects that do not have a strong interest in your products or services is just a waste of time and energy for your organization, even more so if they are unlikely to contribute considerably to earnings in any case. Empower your sales team to evaluate more quickly whether your prospects are a good fit for the products or services your organization sells. Otherwise, you're squandering money, time, and resources on ineffective prospects, negatively harming your bottom line and impeding your business's transition to more sustainable practices.

6) Proceed as follows

Adopting a sustainable sale strategy with no tangible results constitutes cheating. This technique will increase customer distrust, which is difficult to overcome. The guiding idea of sustainable selling is to live and demonstrate your ethics. Consider creating a newsletter outlining your business's environmental goals. Some sort of digest volume or social media post — anything to keep your clients informed about your progress toward meeting your sustainability goals.

INNOVATIVE AND NEW WAYS OF SELLING AND MARKETING

Beth Comstock, a former General Electric vice president, famously stated; Marketing is a never-ending task. This is referred to as perpetual motion. Every day, we must innovate.

Superior marketing equates to improved brand visibility, which should result in more sales. When expressed in these terms, the advertising equation appears straightforward, but this is not the case. There are several methods for attracting clients to a product, and in a constantly changing business, what effectively worked in the past may no longer be feasible in the future. Advertisements in print, on television, and on billboards no longer have the same clout as they did in past generations. Protracted films, fabricated reviews, and pop-up advertisements have begun to vanish.

As traditional marketing tactics have been phased out or are being phased out, new marketing tools and strategies have stepped in to fill the void. As with the individuals it aims to attract, marketing is continuously evolving.

1) Launch a referral program

If you want to rapidly grow your following, you should explore referral marketing. This is a straightforward method in which you enlist the assistance of customers in promoting your goods. It's a straightforward notion, yet most startups I've encountered underutilize it. It's critical to employ because 92% of people value personal advice more than any other sort of marketing.

You want your consumers to be thrilled to spread the word about your startup and to promote it aggressively. To accomplish this efficiently, avoid starting from scratch with a referral scheme. After all, other businesses have already done the legwork for you.

2) Utilize retargeting campaigns

You are probably already familiar with retargeting. However, if you're unfamiliar, retargeting ads are a type of paid display advertising, similar to Google Adwords display ads, that are displayed to people who have previously visited your website or contact in your database (such as a prospective consumer or a current customer). Retargeting makes use of cookies to track your online audience anonymously throughout the web after they leave your site. If a visitor leaves your site without converting after reading a particular blog post, retargeting advertisements on Facebook, Twitter, and/or Google can be used to lure these same visitors into viewing another blog post on your site on the same subject.

Typically, less than 2% of your website visitors convert on their first visit before leaving. Retargeting enables you to focus on the remaining 98 percent by encouraging visitors who have already visited your site to return and convert.

Traditionally, retargeting advertising was used to market things. However, directing readers to your blog content, which has conversion prospects, might be equally successful.

3) Concentrate on popular items

Keep in mind that you must walk with time and trends if you wish to survive in this drastic competitive market; you must be willing to walk with time and trends in order to understand that customers are the king of the business, and you must concentrate on that your specific requirements and preferences.

Simultaneously, because your needs change over time, you must also adapt things to your tastes.

4) Provide a free or discounted product/service

Similar to the lead magnets discussed previously, providing something for free or at a reduced price is an impressive approach to attract new clients. Depending on your type business model, you may also be able to acquire market share by taking a loss. There are countless variations on this particular theme that can be utilized to create leads, sales, and referrals, among other things. Launch discounts have been a huge success for e-commerce shops in particular.

5) Hold a contest

If you want your startup to develop rapidly, consider holding a contest. While most people frequently dismiss contests as a sham method of acquiring new users, this is precisely the strategy employed by some of the most successful startups of the last decade. YouTube has grown to be the world's largest video-sharing website by offering a free iPod Nano to users who upload videos and invite friends on a daily basis. If you want to scale your startup quickly, this is an excellent place to begin.

The difference is that contests are much easier to handle now since tools that did not exist when YouTube began are available. In today's social media world, one of the ideal venues to run a contest that will accelerate your growth is Facebook.

WHAT IS BRANDING ALL ABOUT, AND WHY IS IT IMPORTANT?

A distinctive brand can have a significant influence on your bottom line, providing you with a competitive edge and enabling you to gain and retain customers at a fraction of the expense. In the fast-paced world of e-commerce, where new businesses (and thus new competitors) emerge daily, an established brand can be an invaluable tool for attracting customers and generating profits.

Whether you invest time and effort in developing an attention-grabbing brand or ignore it entirely, your business still has a brand. It may, however, be entirely different from how you want to be perceived.

By carefully constructing your brand through stories, relationships, marketing messages, and visual assets, you can shape your customers' expectations and forge a bond that transcends the buying and selling relationship.

WHAT IS BRANDING?

Marketing is concerned with developing strategies, tactics, methods, and solutions for promoting the services or goods of your firm to potential clients. However, branding is all about establishing a relationship between you and your target clients. Branding actively shapes and differentiates your brand identity from the competitors. It aids in the buyer's decision to choose your services or products over competitors.

Numerous small businesses make the error of overlooking branding initiatives because they view themselves as a business rather than a brand. They trust that brands are the big fish in the pond, with large resources and national recognition. Small firms, resigned to their alleged minnow status, do little more than produce a cute logo and some fancy business cards.

However, branding is critical for businesses of all sizes because it boosts brand value, serves as a guide and motivator for staff, and makes new customer acquisition easier.

Consider the following aspects while developing a good brand:

- Design of a brand (colors, fonts, packaging, themes, etc.)
- Social media presence
- Corporate culture and the surrounding environment
- The product's quality and cost
- Website development and marketing
- Mottos and catchphrases
- Customer support

Apart from these, there are more variables that contribute to the development of a strong brand, including the message, notoriety, tone, philosophy, and overall personality of the organization.

WHY IS THE BRAND IMPORTANT FOR YOUR BUSINESS?

Many small firms fail to capitalize on the numerous opportunities that a good brand presents. You may believe that branding is only important for major corporations with a global consumer base, such as Apple or Nike. However, this is not true! Small business branding is as critical. A strong online brand presence may benefit any firm.

. . .

1) The brand contributes to the development of your reputation

A strong and consistent brand image (which is frequently initiated by a well-designed logo) will aid in the establishment of your business. It aids customers in remembering, recognizing, and advising you. An excellent logo should be strong and simple to recall, immediately making the proper impression on your target audience.

Your logo should be prominently shown on your website, social media profiles, business cards, physical location (if applicable), and printed promotional materials.

2) The brand establishes trust

When a business presents itself professionally, and there is social proof that its products and services are of high quality, potential customers will develop trust in the business and feel more comfortable handing over their hard-earned money.

3) Customer loyalty

Once a customer recognizes and purchases a product or service, a strong brand will entice them to return. A good company with superior products and strong branding strikes all the right chords with customers. In the long run, this will boost consumer loyalty. Apple, which has one of the most successful brand histories in the world, is an excellent example of customer loyalty. He's developed a devoted following by establishing an emotional connection with his clientele. Customer loyalty is a significant factor in Apple's market dominance.

4) Branding may boost employee pride and satisfaction

When a person works for a reputable brand and genuinely believes in what the brand stands for, he or she will be more content with their work and proud of their accomplishments. They'll be pleased to tell their friends where they work, they'll feel more secure with your name on their CV, and they'll feel more connected (which will make them less tempted by your competitors!). By branding your workplace and providing promotional items for employees to utilize, you can assist in strengthening your brand and the values it symbolizes.

5) Incorporate emotion

If you give consumers a reason to care about and connect with your brand, you've given them a reason to buy. Because the majority of individuals make purchasing decisions based on emotion rather than reasoning, every time your prospects see your brand, you instill an emotion in them.

Regardless of size, the most successful businesses have established themselves as industry leaders through the development of a strong brand. And by focusing on generating value customer experiences, these businesses can easily convert customers into brand ambassadors.

3
WHAT IS IT THAT MAKE THEM DECIDE

By considering multiple options and deciding on the best course of action, decision-making assists managers and other business professionals resolve difficulties. Marketing theory is frequently the motivating reason behind business decisions regarding their marketing initiatives. To successfully apply marketing science to your organization, however, you must first have a meaningful understanding of your consumer.

At first glance, the process of customer decision-making may appear mysterious. Why do people acquire things? It's too simple to oversimplify the motivation for purchasing behaviors to address the customer's basic needs. However, their reasons at each level are anchored in fundamental psychological and physical requirements. Understanding this premise is critical for simplifying the decision-making process for customers.

UNDERSTANDING CUSTOMERS' DECISION-MAKING PROCESS

Consumer Decision Processes (often referred to as Buyer Decision Processes) refer to the decision-making stages that a consumer goes through before, during, and after purchasing a product or service. Consumer behavior has long been a popular marketing topic. Understanding how and why customers behave in specific ways while making purchasing decisions enables businesses to enhance their marketing efforts and increase their market share.

Consumer behavior has long been a popular marketing topic, as understanding how and why customers behave in specific ways while making purchasing decisions enables businesses to enhance their marketing efforts and increase their market share. However, before you can learn how to influence a customer's purchasing process to make it easier, you must first grasp it. Therefore, six distinct processes and the associated tasks have been broken down to keep things easy.

1) Need Recognition

This is the first phase of the Consumer Decision Process in which the consumer determines what the problem or need is and, consequently, what product or type of product would be able to meet the demand. It is sometimes seen as the first and most critical phase in the process since consumers would generally refrain from considering a product purchase if they do not identify a problem or need.

Internal or external factors might elicit a craving. Internal stimuli refer to a consumer's subjective perception, such as hunger or thirst.

· · ·

2) Information Search

Once a need has been identified, the potential customer may seek information to identify and evaluate different items, services, and outlets that will satisfy that need. This information may originate through family, friends, personal observation, or other sources such as Consumer Reports, salespeople, or the news media. The promotional component of the marketer's offering is designed to educate the consumer and aid them in their problem-solving process. In some circumstances, the consumer already possesses the necessary information due to prior purchases and consumption. Negative encounters and dissatisfaction might sabotage repeat purchases. For example, a consumer in need of tires may consult the local newspaper or solicit recommendations from friends. If they've previously purchased tires and were satisfied, they may return to the same dealer and buy the same brand.

Additionally, information search can help uncover new requirements. For example, as a tire buyer gathers knowledge, they may conclude that the real issue is a requirement for a new car. The apparent requirement may have shifted at this stage, necessitating a new informative search. Consumers must engage in both mental and physical activity in order to make decisions and achieve desired outcomes in the marketplace.

3) Evaluating Alternatives

During the alternative evaluation stage, the consumer rates all accessible products on a scale of certain criteria. The third stage of the Consumer Buying Decision Process is the evaluation of alternatives. Consumers evaluate all of their brands and selections on a scale of traits that are capable of delivering the advantage sought by the customer during this stage.

Consumers' evoked set of brands and goods represents the alternatives they examine during the problem-solving process.

At this point, your customers have conducted due diligence and determined what they require to close the gap. Additionally, they have established a set of criteria for what they desire in a product or service. They examine, mark, and file away every review, advertisement, and marketing material they come across.

4) Purchase Decision

After extensive searching and evaluation, or possibly very little, shoppers must eventually decide whether to purchase. Anything marketers can do to streamline the purchasing process will appeal to shoppers. This may include fewer clicks to complete the online checkout process, shorter queue times, and streamlined payment alternatives. When it comes to advertising, marketers can also recommend the appropriate size for a given purpose or the appropriate wine to pair with a particular dish. Occasionally, multiple-choice circumstances can be packaged together and marketed as a single unit. For instance, travel brokers frequently combine tour packages with flight and hotel reservations.

To perform more effectively as a marketer at this point of the purchasing process, a seller must have answers to numerous questions concerning consumer shopping behavior. For instance, how much time and effort is the consumer willing to devote to product shopping? What variables influence the consumer's decision to make a purchase? Are there any restrictions or limitations that would prevent or postpone the purchase? The obvious place to begin is by providing a basic product, price, and location information via labels, advertising, personal selling, and public relations. Additionally, product samples, promotions, and rebates may serve as an additional incentive to purchase.

5) Post-Purchase Behavior

Post-purchase behavior occurs when the customer evaluates his or her satisfaction with a purchase. Following-Purchase Behavior Post-buy behavior is the stage of the consumer decision-making process at which the customer determines whether he or she is satisfied or dissatisfied with a purchase. How a customer feels about a purchase has a huge impact on whether he will buy the goods again or examine other products in the brand's portfolio. A client can also influence the buying decisions of others because he or she will likely feel compelled to communicate his or her thoughts regarding the purchase.

At this stage, cognitive dissonance, another form of buyer's regret, is widespread. This is when the customer may experience psychological strain or anxiety following the purchase. For instance, the buyer may feel driven to doubt if he made the correct choice. Additionally, consumers may be exposed to advertising for a competing product or brand, which may cast doubt on the product they have chosen. Additionally, a consumer may have a change of heart and determine that he no longer requires this particular product.

HOW DO YOU WIN IN DECISION-MAKING?

Today's buyers are bombarded with an infinite number of possibilities, resulting in severe decision fatigue. As a result, many of them become frustrated when shopping, make fast selections, or opt for the "no choice" option, deferring a purchase decision.

As option overload becomes a genuine concern for both

customers and organizations across industries, an increasing number of firms are investigating ways to assist their visitors in discovering, selecting, and deciding on the appropriate product to purchase. Offering a seamless and rapid path to the appropriate product is not an option. If you do not take action, someone else will.

Recognizing the detrimental effects of option overload on your organization and taking action to address them enables you to differentiate and improve your company's overall perception.

1) Make an investment in knowledge management software

In a world where problems and judgments are becoming increasingly precise, the support that knowledge base software can provide genuinely reigns supreme. Not only does this provide direct access to solutions for your consumer, but it also does so considerably more quickly and efficiently. With solutions explained in separate modules and call center executives no longer intercepted, clients now have access to a selection of simply understandable options that nearly always point them in the proper direction.

2) Data collection

In order for the consumer to collect data, data must be supplied. This is an area where shops may demonstrate their expertise and earn a customer's trust by displaying informative content. Because a store worker will not always be accessible to provide customers with the information they require, you can build instructional messages that provide just enough information to empower them to make their own decisions.

· · ·

3) Reasonable decisions are preferred decisions

According to renowned psychologist Jerome Bruner, individuals remember 80% of what they see, 20% of what they read, and just 10% of what they hear. If you want your clients to make informed choices, you must give them information in the most understandable form possible — images. Utilize visual aids that are rich in images and graphics to help your clients understand solutions. This aids in their comprehension of the information and raises the likelihood that they will choose the best solution for themselves.

Additionally, with the emergence of new technologies such as augmented and virtual reality, the screen is no longer a barrier to conveying your message effectively. The more succinct your message, the more obvious the correct choice will be to your buyer.

4) Live Chat

Live Chat is the digital equivalent of a customer approaching a sales associate in-store and soliciting guidance.

To summarize, clients do not want to feel as if they are speaking with a robot. Providing an authentic and useful live chat experience will not only assist your consumer in locating the appropriate product or service but will also instill confidence in your company.

5) Copywriting

The art of selling items or increasing awareness through the use of the appropriate words in the appropriate sequence. Traditionally, copywriters were responsible for producing advertisements for television, magazines, and outbound media; now, in the digital age, these responsibilities have expanded to include website copy, social media, blog entries, Google AdWords, and a host of other digital content.

As you are likely aware, the purpose of copywriting is to persuade your reader to act, i.e., to believe in your idea. Whether you're trying to convince them to purchase a product or service or subscribe to an email list, many people understand what copywriting is. However, very few people know how to do it well. Understanding the psychology of your reader is an excellent method to improve your copywriting.

If you understand why people buy and what inspires them to buy, you can use this information to your benefit. According to research, almost 95% of our purchasing decisions are made subconsciously (Zaltman 2020). This is why marketers invest so much time and money in attempting to emotionally connect people with their products.

By demonstrating how your products have benefited actual individuals. Your clients will feel more connected to your business and will be more eager to share the news about it.

6) Act

Once a customer has opted to purchase, it is up to the store to make their purchasing alternatives crystal obvious and to eliminate any friction in the last phases of the process. Assuming the item is too large to carry, you can purchase it in-store and have it transported to your home for free. Alternatively, have a sales employee volunteer to assist you in carrying it out of the store. Alternatively, offer a simple transaction close to the product's placement in the store to avoid the consumer queuing at the main point of sale. Consider each consumer's wants towards the conclusion of their purchasing experience to enhance the pleasure of the transaction.

HOW DO YOU MAKE DECISION EASIER?

The manner in which you provide something to individuals is also a critical component of a business strategy. Without clients, it's quite self-evident that you don't have a business. However, acquiring new clients does not occur automatically. You must devise strategies to contact them, entice them, facilitate their decision-making, and keep them coming back for more. Your firm requires a marketing strategy that focuses on customer acquisition and revenue growth. Attracting new clients is not a natural process. Here are a few things you can do to make it easier for customers to make purchasing decisions.

1) Provide a customized experience through live engagement

How do you earn the trust and confidence of your customers and make their patronage easier? By assisting your clients. And how are you going to do it? One of the more effective methods is the use of live engagement technologies. By personalizing messages and utilizing live customer engagement, you can assist your clients throughout their purchasing journey. With the tools, you may increase client satisfaction by providing immediate personalized service.

Co-browsing aids in the completion of complex transactions such as form filling, product demonstrations, and customer onboarding. Agents may examine the customer's screen with a single click and coach them through the appropriate action or complex query.

Businesses can have personalized interactions with clients and give a tailored service using engagement tools such as video chat and voice chat. These individualized dialogues foster client trust and are one of the tactics for acquiring new customers.

2) Price

This pertains to your service and product price plan and the impact it will have on your customers. You should determine how much your customers are willing to pay, the markup necessary to cover overheads, profit margins, and payment options, as well as other charges. To encourage clients to patronize your business and maintain your competitive edge, you may also want to explore discounting and seasonal pricing.

3) Be where your customers are

On average, businesses with a great omnichannel strategy retain 89 percent of their customers, compared to 33 percent for those with a weak omnichannel approach (Dennis 2018). The omnichannel strategy entails delving into your customer's life-cycle and engaging with them across all touch-points.

Customers can contact you via a variety of channels, including your website, social media, messaging applications, mobile, call center, online forums, and physical stores.

4) Physical evidence

This category includes everything your clients see when they connect with your firm. This comprises the actual environment in which your product or service is provided, the layout or interior design of your facility, your packaging, and your branding.

Physical evidence can also apply to your staff's appearance and behavior. Consider how the layout, fixtures, and signage of your store may help you create your brand, simplify customer decision-making, and enhance your sales.

5) Understand your customers' expectations

Gather as much information as possible about your clients. Determine what your customers want, what they buy, and how frequently they buy. When attempting to comprehend their requirements, it may be beneficial to learn about their lifestyle, work, and interests. If you want to give excellent customer service, you need to understand the customer's needs and how to meet them. It is critical for you to understand how your clients anticipate you will address their demands.

The expected degree of service varies by the marketplace, industry, and, to a lesser extent, a consumer group. Conduct market research and then target your audience with the appropriate message to ascertain what your customers anticipate from your organization.

PSYCHOLOGY BEHIND MIND MAKING

Psychology is referred to as the study of behavior and the mind from a scientific perspective. Additionally, it relates to the application of knowledge, which can be utilized to comprehend events, treat mental health disorders, and enhance educational, employment, and interpersonal interactions. The subject straddles the divide between applied, pedagogical, and theoretical science.

It's strange that the mind exists at all. How could something as insubstantial and noble as mind or consciousness come from three pounds of gelatinous pudding inside the skull? Nobody is certain. Additionally, while the mind is generated by the brain, it can function independently of the brain. Indeed, the mind has the ability to alter the brain.

Customer psychology refers to the internal thoughts that customers have about a brand or product. Their state of mind is their psychology; you must master it in order to be successful and lure people to your brand's website. Each day, individuals make an unlimited number of choices. From simple life decisions such as what to eat or the route they take to work to more complex ones such as changing careers, sending their children to a particular school, or deciding whether to remain in a romantic relationship. The purpose of this discipline is to better understand why consumers make specific choices about their time, effort, and money when acquiring items and services.

Numerous studies have been conducted to determine how people's choices and subsequent outcomes affect their emotional well-being and life satisfaction. Simply put, when people feel empowered and make positive choices, they feel better about themselves and their lives, resulting in increased psychological well-being (Dinardi, 2019).

Psychology allows people to have a better understanding of how the mind and body interact. This understanding can help in decision-making and the avoidance of potentially stressful circumstances. It can aid in time management, goal setting and achievement, and productive living.

As a business owner, you're probably aware that creating buyer personas is a necessary first step in developing successful marketing campaigns. This becomes much more critical when considering the primary psychological factors in a lead's decision-making process. You should have a firm grasp on all of the psychological effects that your buyer encounters in order to design your marketing accordingly.

HOW TO BUILD LONG-LASTING RELATIONSHIPS WITH YOUR CUSTOMERS?

A common error made by business owners, particularly those new to the field, is to focus nearly completely on lead generation and customer acquisition. And while it is critical to understand how to grow your consumer base, it is not the only factor to consider. Existing customers are equally as critical as new ones. Indeed, they may be more critical in the long run, as cultivating long-term connections with clients provides numerous long-term benefits. As a result, you should surely incorporate it into your business strategy.

1) Know Your Customers

Are you aware of your customers? If you do, fantastic! Because many clients prefer to work with firms with which they may establish a personal connection rather than with a faceless organization. When you have the chance to speak with customers directly, take the time to inquire about their interests and issues, as well as to solicit feedback on your work. Furthermore, do not be scared to take notes! You want to ensure that you act on the information provided by the consumer and that you have a thorough grasp of their experience. Additionally, remembering that personal knowledge the next time you speak with them contributes significantly to building a favorable relationship.

2) Demonstrate the desired behavior

How you treat your employees sets an example for how they should treat your customers. If you're constantly looking for ways to save money, your employees may believe they're not allowed to offer discounts or add value in other ways, which can go a long way toward exceeding customer expectations.

3) Be proactive

Keep clients informed about your products, new releases, articles/links of topical relevance, and anything else that may pique their interest. A newsletter sent via email is an excellent way to accomplish this. This eliminates the need for clients to follow you on social media, as you will appear straight in their inboxes. Additionally, whenever possible, respond to comments on your blog or elsewhere online.

4) Surprise Customers

It's easy to delight your customers! Simply provide them with more than they anticipate. That entails going above and beyond your first commitment. Consider surprising clients on their birthdays with a gift. Alternatively, you might send a modest token of appreciation to a loyal customer. The present does not need to be extreme. A Starbucks gift card, a discount code for their next purchase, or even a complimentary sample of your product expresses gratitude without being excessive.

5) Host live events

Host live events as a means to connect with customers on a more personal level. Create an event to express your gratitude or host a retreat for some of your best customers to provide feedback and get to know you better.

6) Always Be Honest with Customers

Establishing a reputation for dependability, honesty, and integrity is critical for developing good customer connections. Customer trust is just as critical as the items or services you sell. Maintain an honest, open, and real relationship with your clientele. If you are unable to deliver on a commitment, notify them immediately. Successful long-term customer relationships are built on trust and openness.

4
WHAT IS SO IMPORTANT ABOUT DELIVERY

The foundation of a sales plan is a viable delivery route. It is improbable that the brand will be able to get its items to the end consumer in the absence of a proper distribution channel. In the case of newly launched, innovative, or service-heavy products, these are especially crucial. The world is expanding rapidly; thus, a company's distribution strategy is crucial to its competitive advantage, in addition to the product's accessibility and availability. Most organizations today target their clients far and wide any place on Earth. Additionally, they attempt to extend into other markets to increase their turnover. Therefore, distribution channels are the most important aspect of any company's marketing initiatives, allowing you to contact customers in a manner that maximizes revenue and brand exposure.

CHOOSING THE RIGHT DELIVERY PARTNER

Whether you own a clothes business or a restaurant, you must seek ways to service your consumers better. Numerous firms rely on online sales to respond to modern problems. More so now that cashless and contactless transactions are desired.

There are numerous elements that influence a company's distribution channel, including the presence of established competitors and the market's demand for its products. Each of these aspects influences the decision-making process, and clarity is necessary before selecting a channel. Choosing the appropriate online ordering system is the first step if you plan to accept online orders. Prior to making a decision, you must take into account a number of aspects.

1) Cost

As an online business owner, you're certainly aware that the delivery charges for outsourcing shipping operations may add up rapidly; therefore, you must be able to calculate your delivery expenses in relation to the value they bring to your firm.

This can be tough because it is difficult to assign a quantifiable value to the improvement of customer experience. While boosting sales will almost always be your primary objective, you must also monitor and measure your success in other (less quantitative) ways. You can determine the value offered to your business by your chosen courier services by reading customer reviews or conducting a brief survey to determine how satisfied your customers are with the shipping experience.

2) Track record

When examining potential partners, one of the most crucial things to consider is what they have accomplished. Find out what others are saying about a distributor; this will tell you a great deal about its services and capacity to achieve outcomes.

Reputation and client satisfaction are crucial markers of a company's suitability as a business partner and potential worth to your organization. In conjunction with a history of retained vendors, these are reassuring characteristics to look for in a prospective delivery partner.

3) Speed

Speed is arguably one of the most significant and prevalent deciding elements when selecting a delivery service. For many firms, delivery speed is crucial. Even if the timing is typically not a concern, you never know when delivery may need to be rushed. Consider each company's average delivery speed and the range of possible delivery speeds. Some may only be able to provide normal and expedited shipping, but others will offer a variety of delivery speeds to meet your every demand.

4) The reach potential

Customers and potential customers must have easy access to the chosen channel. If you sell locally, find a retailer or distributor who is familiar with the local market. If you are expanding and wish to sell your products in more states, you should select a distribution network that covers your desired markets. With the advent of the Internet, businesses of all sizes are now able to sell their products on a global scale. The cost of establishing a website that can be accessed by any client with Internet access is much lower than the expense of establishing or managing a global distribution network.

5) Product

Perishable commodities require swift movement and a

shorter distribution route. For durable and conventional items, a longer and more diverse distribution channel may be required. Whereas direct distribution to the consumer or industrial user may be preferable for custom-made products.

Also, we offer the shortest path for technical products needing professional selling and customer service talent. High-value products are marketed directly by traveling sales teams, without the need for middlemen.

6) Attitude towards care

If you are transporting sensitive materials, fragile products, or something that must arrive in good shape, your courier's attitude toward care is crucial. There are several horror stories of couriers who mishandle fragile products, leaving them broken upon delivery, or who use repeated truck changes to minimize costs, hence increasing the likelihood that something will break during delivery. When making your decision, be sure to inquire about the company's approach to caring for your delivery and to read their evaluations.

7) Skill level of service providers

You want your clients to receive the best service possible. When dealing with customers through a third-party distribution channel, this is difficult. If you sell high-value, sophisticated items to business customers, you require salespeople with excellent product expertise and relationship-building skills.

If your customer base is tiny, a direct sales team may be the ideal answer. If you have a significant number of company clients across the nation, you should seek out a distributor network that sells similar products. They will have the expertise and knowledge to sell your products, especially if you provide product training to their sales crew.

Marketers closely monitor the channels used by competitors. Distribution of a company's products may frequently benefit from the use of similar channels. Sometimes, marketers ignore channels utilized by competitors on purpose. For instance, a corporation may forgo the retail store channel (used by competitors) in favor of door-to-door sales (where there is no competition).

9) Tracking capability

How vital is it for you to always know where your shipment is? Are you going to hand over your packages without knowing where they traveled? Or will your courier be able to provide you with complete and detailed tracking features that allow you to know exactly where your package is and has been, with minute-by-minute updates?

10) Integrity and openness

When collaborating with a firm, it is essential that they are truthful in all aspects, especially when you're entrusting them with the crucial task of delivering your goods.

You want complete candor on any problems or delays, and you should have faith that your courier service is actively striving to find a solution. This kind of honesty is invaluable to you and your clients. When the recipient inquires as to why their gift has not arrived, you can provide them with a detailed explanation. Identifying a reliable delivery partner is simple if you know the telltale indications. Their continuous customer service should be their main selling point, but it should not be the only one.

IMPORTANCE OF CHOOSING THE RIGHT DELIVERY SERVICE

For business owners, superior delivery service is vital for retaining customers. An important proportion of the world's population is now shopping online, with the number of digital purchasers increasing annually and consumer behavior changing dramatically by 2020. (**Coral, 2022**). The ideal delivery service for businesses is one that helps them save money and boosts productivity and efficiency when it comes to making many deliveries each day. This improves the consumer experience for those who can plan their day around the delivery time.

1) Enhance quality and reputation

Customer retention is essential for success. Maintaining good standards is crucial for retaining client loyalty, which will enhance your company's brand and attract new consumers. Two-thirds of consumers believe that substandard delivery is the worst thing that can go wrong with shopping. The majority of clients utilize eCommerce services for their convenience, but if deliveries are late or incorrect, they may not return to make additional purchases, resulting in a loss of confidence and reputation.

2) Facilitate your work

Delivery services are incredibly simple to use. This service eliminates the need to visit the post office in order to send and receive mail and shipments. You can have a courier deliver or collect the packages on your behalf. This will allow staff to focus on their jobs and do more work for your company. The majority of courier services now offer online management tools. With these capabilities, you may set delivery and pickup times, among other things, making this service even more convenient.

3) Minimize time and effort

Having a robust delivery management procedure in place will help boost your company's efficiency and reduce the time and effort spent on deliveries. To assure that all the process goes as smoothly as possible, assign specific duties to specific persons and ensure that everyone is aware of how their contribution affects the overall operation. Utilize a reputable delivery management company to oversee the delivery process and guarantee on-time delivery to your consumers. This will allow your employees to devote more time to other elements of the organization.

4) Quick delivery

The delivery company you select should offer quick delivery, which has numerous advantages so that your packages and documents reach their destination swiftly. You can inform your courier of the package's delivery deadline in order to ensure that it arrives on time. For even quicker service, you can select one-hour delivery for time-sensitive packages. With these excellent services, you have greater control over your parcel delivery, thereby increasing the efficiency of your organization.

5) It allows you to keep up with the competition

As delivery services have vastly improved in recent years, clients now demand a quick, economic, and problem-free experience. If your company is unable to match these requirements, they will easily turn to your competition. Consequently, offering a flawless delivery service has become essential for keeping up with the competition. It is also a chance to distinguish yourself from your competition if you can create a service that functions properly and is effective.

6) It is linked to customer service

Delivery is currently linked to customer service. Therefore, clients want you to go above and above when it comes to shipping their orders. Poor delivery service is regarded as poor customer service, which is never good for business. Therefore, if you do not already view delivery as a significant aspect of customer service, you could be losing a substantial amount of revenue.

WHY IS SPEED IMPORTANT DURING THE DELIVERY OF PRODUCTS?

Simply said, timely delivery is essential since no one likes waiting anymore. People are more impatient. The allure of waiting for a delivery to come after an internet shopping spree has diminished. Even a few years ago, it was considered usual to wait for seven to ten business days for an online order to arrive. However, due to technological advancements, same-day and next-day delivery are now the standards.

Therefore, customers today desire speedier service and are even willing to pay extra for it. Regardless of whether you are delivering a service or product, the turnaround time must be as quick as feasible. Customers have a tendency to become impatient within a short period of time, and delayed delivery services can cause a client to cancel an order and seek out a competitor.

1) It is convenient for your customers

Anything that offers convenience wins over the hearts of numerous customers. Likewise, if you deliver orders quickly, it will be incredibly convenient for the people you serve. Customers despise having to wait a long time for their orders to arrive. Worse even, if the order is to be distributed locally, they become easily angry if it takes months to arrive when it should arrive within a day. Therefore, if you are dealing with local customers, guarantee that the order is delivered as quickly as possible, preferably within hours or a day. In addition, overseas clients should not have lengthy shipment delays.

2) Competing effectively

If a consumer has a pressing need for an item and can find it on both your website and that of a rival, they are more likely to choose the website that offers expedited shipping. Whether it's a gift for a forgotten birthday or a replacement for a broken item, there are a variety of reasons why consumers may need something as soon as possible; therefore, it's beneficial to offer this option at checkout.

When you offer fast delivery, your firm becomes competitive not only with other online merchants but also with brick-and-mortar establishments. There will always be individuals who need things quickly, which is one reason why certain merchants remain in business. However, if you can give essentially the same speed without requiring customers to drive to the store and park, you open up an entirely new market.

· · ·

3) Increase in credibility

When your consumers are satisfied with your service, they will spread the word to others. Same-day delivery is an excellent method for boosting client satisfaction. They will perceive that you care about their wants and are willing to go out of your way to deliver their products as quickly as possible. Consequently, you will appear more credible and professional, which will do wonders for your brand image.

4) Enhances your company's reputation

Word-of-mouth is extremely persuasive. A customer who has had a negative experience with a firm's delivery system is likely to speak poorly of that company. On the other hand, a client who is satisfied with your company's delivery services is likely to refer you to others. As a result, your company's reputation and brand are strengthened. In addition, your brand increases as an increasing number of clients suggest others to your organization due to the quick turnaround time. In no time at all, your firm will be able to scale up without incurring a significant amount of marketing expenses, as your customers will suggest you to others. This is a win for any business.

5) Building loyal customers

In terms of marketing, it is much more expensive to acquire new customers than it is to maintain existing ones. Offering incentives such as same-day delivery could encourage brand loyalty. It implies that people know exactly where to go when they need something quickly; therefore, when time is of the matter, they will choose you over the competitors.

· · ·

6) Improved inventory management system

Why stack merchandise in your warehouse if you have a better inventory management system? Not only is it a waste of space, but also of time and effort to find a way to organize everything. With speed delivery, manufacturing and sales work in tandem, so you do not need to create a complicated inventory system for your bursting warehouse. Concentrate your energy and time on more essential things. You can enjoy a wide variety of benefits by providing your consumers with expedited courier delivery services. In today's world of quick gratification, it is an ever-increasing necessity. Not only will your customers enjoy it, but so will you.

IMPORTANCE OF CONSISTENCY IN CUSTOMER SERVICE

As a business expert, you have likely heard innumerable business ideas over the years, whether from professional colleagues, conferences, or home-study books. It might be challenging to run a successful business, but if you prioritize consistency across all platforms of your day-to-day operations, you will find yourself on the path to success. By emphasizing consistency in your business, you can ensure that your customers and clients understand who you are, what your focus is, and how your products and services may benefit them.

There are numerous reasons why achieving consistency should be a priority. Consider these factors when deciding how much work you wish to invest in developing this principle in your corporate environment.

1) Responsibility

This is likely the most obvious issue but also the one that is most likely to be neglected. It is fundamentally human to deflect responsibility and assign blame when the desired objective is not achieved. By establishing consistency around work objectives and goals and applying practices that keep you on track, you build accountability not only for yourself but also for your team.

2) Appearance of organization

Workplaces where there is stability appear more organized than those where there is frequent change. For instance, if your staff uses the same way to record their task completion and request time off, it would look to them that you have greater control over the organization. This image of structure might improve employees' perceptions of the company and give them the impression that it is more stable.

3) Differentiates your brand

It is crucial to be heard above the advertising noise, and consistency helps a buyer grasp what differentiates your brand from the competition, particularly when you emphasize your USP. A unique selling proposition (or USP) is a factor that distinguishes a product from its competitors, such as the highest quality, lowest price, or exclusivity. A USP can be defined as "what you have that your competitors do not." Consider Walmart and Target as an illustration. They are both powerful merchants with similar concepts and slogans, but they are easily distinguishable in-store and in their advertisements. Walmart emphasizes customers' desire to save money through their "Save Money. Live Better." motto and "everyday low price" advertising. Target, on the other hand, emphasizes quality over pricing with its "Expect more. Payless" slogan and its usage of renowned designers on a regular basis. The slogans are easy to recall, and clients will immediately recognize which store is being advertised based on the wording.

4) Clarity

In addition to accountability, another inescapable result of consistency is clarity. How often have you arrived at work with no idea what you were supposed to accomplish that day? This has a negative influence on your mood as you get increasingly anxious as you try to catch up on the chores you didn't do the night before and are constantly confronted with new assignments.

5) Increased comfort levels

Although some individuals are tolerant of frequent change, the vast majority prefer stability. When your processes and procedures are standardized, your workplace will likely appear less chaotic and more under control. By establishing a consistent environment, you can assist your employees and clients feel at ease in the workplace.

6) Confidence

When you have a clear mind and are driven, it is natural for your confidence to increase. You will become considerably more forceful, self-assured, and confident in your selections. There is a clear distinction between confidence and arrogance, so please do not mistake the two. Nothing is more appealing for current and prospective clients than someone who is confident in their abilities, approach, and demeanor. You will naturally instill trust through your tone and body language.

. . .

7) Increased employee understanding

Keeping up with laws and processes that are continuously evolving can be mentally taxing. If you create a consistent plan for your workplace and deviate from it infrequently, it will be easier for your employees to understand their job responsibilities and your expectations for them.

HOW TO MEET THE DELIVERY EXPECTATIONS OF THE CUSTOMER

Delivering means keeping your brand's promises. It entails ensuring that your products and services can meet the needs and requirements of your consumers. Due to shifting consumer expectations, it is evident that fast and free shipping is no longer merely desirable fulfillment options. Not providing online shoppers with a variety of appealing fulfillment options is now frequently a deal-breaker. Due to the propagation of social media, these customer expectations are now frequently made public. However, it remains difficult to identify them and develop a viable solution. You might even lose sleep over the prospect of meeting and exceeding these customer expectations.

Here are essential components of delivery and methods for developing a consistent, dependable delivery procedure.

1) Communicate at each and every stage

After clicking "purchase now," your customers begin the waiting game. Will my order arrive in due time for my event, or will it arrive at all? And will I be home to sign?

Customers want business owners to alleviate their tension

through effective communication. Inform your clients that you had received their order, when it was shipped, and when they may expect to receive it.

2) Custom packaging

Your packaging is the first thing your buyer sees, even before the product itself. As a result, many business owners opt for specialized shipping boxes. By partnering with the right shipping company, you cannot only make a favorable impression but also acquire new clients and maintain existing ones.

3) Consistency

Whether you have a standardized or customized delivery process, your objective is to achieve output consistency. Consistency is essential for establishing and sustaining a positive brand reputation. It corresponds to consistency and predictability in your delivery procedure. This is crucial for your customers and clients. Consistent delivery of your products and services assists in establishing customer expectations. Your clients and consumers enjoy it when you have a defined and predictable timeframe for carrying out specific tasks (e.g., processing orders or accomplishing projects).

4) Don't forget about returns

We know that delivery capabilities are a major deciding factor for customers when selecting a brand. Although, many business owners have a tendency to be so focused on delivery that they disregard the returns procedure, so losing repeat customers. The same vigilance devoted to delivery via different carriers, communication, and convenience must be applied to the returns process, ensuring that all customers' returns are simple and convenient. Due to an uncertain high street climate, consumer expectations of shops are currently extremely high; thus, losing a customer at the very end of their trip appears like a waste of the hard effort put in at the beginning.

5) Deliver on your promises

If there is a problem with fulfillment, inform your clients promptly and provide a complete refund if they are unwilling to wait. Avoid requiring them to contact you first. Provide your clients with a range of contact options, and make these options evident at the point of sale. Utilize a tracked delivery service so you can provide clients with tracking information to comfort them that their orders are on their way.

6) Underpromise and overdeliver

When attempting to win over customers, it can be tempting to make grand claims. But what happens if you are unable to fulfill your obligations?

You risk not only disappointing your customers but also losing their total confidence. It makes no difference how popular or powerful your brand already is. Your credibility will ultimately be harmed by a lack of delivery follow-up.

In terms of delivery, it is frequently preferable to under-promise and overdeliver. Aim to provide clients with products and services that not only meet but surpass their expectations. By doing such, you provide them with the type of pleasant surprise that is always appreciated.

5

HOW CAN YOU TAKE ADVANTAGE OF CUSTOMERS USING YOUR SOLUTION?

You may not be able to influence the weather or your competition, but you have complete control over the level of customer service you deliver. Therefore, you should constantly devise strategies to impress your customers. Eighty per cent of customers today believe that the experience they have with a business or corporation is equally as significant as its products. The consumer experience is as vital as the product itself. It is not about whose product has superior features or a sleeker user interface. It's about which establishment is simpler to do business with, which corporation makes them feel more valued, and which establishment recognizes them as individuals, not just as assets to the bottom line.

Customer experience entails motivating customers to interact with you and engaging them when they do so that they enjoy the interaction. It takes knowing your clients and valuing that information within your firm. If you're comparing your company to others and wondering why your consumers aren't raving about you, this chapter will teach you a few things to avoid.

Being trustworthy and making sure that the product is

what was promised and more promises are made to be kept, hence the saying, "Don't make a promise you can't keep." In other form, do not make promises you cannot deliver. This is precisely where the majority of brands fail. In their eagerness to get customers, they overpromise. Then they underdeliver once the buyer enters the establishment. Or provide something which was not promised. The brand promise becomes a stinging reminder of what you, the customer, could have enjoyed if the brand had fulfilled its promise. Ultimately, the brand promise boils down to trust, integrity, and following through on commitments. It appears to be so obvious, doesn't it? But few do it well.

WHAT IS BRAND PROMISE?

We are accustomed to referring to a company's total identity as its 'brand' in addition to the products and services it creates and sells. In addition to the products and services offered for sale, a company's brand includes its distinctive approach to business, its values, beliefs, and philosophy. If the company were a person, the brand would be its personality. Because firms are in the business of solving people's problems, each brand makes what we might call a 'brand promise' to consumers. This is not tied to a certain service or product, and it is rarely mentioned explicitly, but it is evident in many of the company's pronouncements and manifestations (especially its advertisements).

What establishes the emotional connection between a customer and a firm is centered on brand promises. However, firms themselves have a propensity to overlook these pledges. What is a brand promise, then? How does it vary from a mission statement or slogan?

A brand promise is a succinct statement or phrase that

describes what a consumer might anticipate from a brand across all touch-points. It may not be explicit or customer-facing. The majority of the time, it is an internal motto shared with employees, investors, and business partners. Rather, a brand promise acts as a company's guiding principle and should inform all elements of its operations, from marketing to customer service. It should be fundamental to your organization, something that remains constant as the business develops and changes. If you have established strong brand identity with clear messaging, your target audience will likely assume or at least grasp the essence of your brand promise.

HOW TO CREATE PROMISES FOR YOUR BRAND?

Every interaction with your organization should be consistent with your brand promise. The customer experience should be uniform across all goods, departments, branches, and locations. Your brand promise is a fundamental component of your brand statement. It can distinguish you and inspire your development. How can you establish a brand promise that will keep your customers coming back for more?

1) Determine how clients perceive your current brand

You must communicate with your customers. You presumably discuss their problems and business with them frequently. It may be personally challenging, but it is perfectly acceptable to inquire about their perceptions of your brand. Ask inquiries such as, "Why are you coming to us instead of going elsewhere?"

- What do you think of our brand? I would love to hear your viewpoint.

- What comes to mind as you contemplate?

Conversations with customers one-on-one will help you empathize with their perspectives, allowing you to see how your brand seems to them. Direct engagement with clients can be quite beneficial for an organization's leader. In-person communication is ideal. Video calls are OK but less useful. Note that you gather as much information from their body language and facial emotions as from their words. Email and text messages are preferable to nothing, but they do not provide a complete experience.

There is no alternative to speaking with customers. Surveys and feedback forms are excellent methods for gaining an overall understanding of how customers perceive a company. However, they frequently attract a minority of very satisfied or angry clients, skewing the data.

2) Know your brand

This is not mean that you must think outside the usual objective of your organization. Not every brand has the resources to make the world a better place, and not every brand should aspire to do so. Each proposed component of a brand promise must satisfy the following conditions:

- It is something you know your business performs better than any other.
- It is something for which consumers and prospects recognize you.
- You are confident that you can give it repeatedly.

If like Wegman's, low prices are the primary reason buyers purchase your brand, you do not need to make quality promises. Knowing your brand (and not lying to yourself) will result in a brand promise upon which your firm may grow.

3) Credibility

If the consumer experience does not align with the brand promise, the brand's value is diminished. Ford Motor Company is an example of a company whose brand promise has not been fulfilled. Throughout the 1980s, Ford's slogan was "Quality is Job One." However, Ford vehicle owners were not impressed, as they often incurred repair costs. It became so terrible that people created their own brand promise for Ford: "Ford— Found On Roadside Broken."

The current brand promise for Ford is "Go Further."

4) Define your target market

Which population do you serve? Which terms would you use to classify them?

Your brand does not cater to every person on earth. If a brand is to be significant, it must target a subset of individuals and address their specific requirements in an exceptional manner. Starbucks caters to coffee connoisseurs. Blizzard caters to players. IBM serves businesses. Entrepreneurs, marketing experts, and designers are served by BMB.

5) Make a guarantee your business can keep

Although not every consumer will have the desired interaction with your brand, you and your coworkers should make every effort to ensure that they do. That entails creating a brand promise that isn't used only for marketing and sales and is well within your organization's means. A brand promise may and should be aspirational; your organization should use it as a growth driver. However, this will be impossible if you cannot fulfill this promise for a significant portion of your audience.

Do not, for example, boast about your customer service if your organization lacks the infrastructure to guarantee that every customer receives excellent service. If you are aware that your colleagues are striving to resolve usability difficulties with your product, don't emphasize its simplicity. These instances may appear obvious, but the underlying message is vital. A brand promise should serve as a target for your company's growth and development. However, it must be an attainable objective. Avoid overpromising to consumers, and you'll position your team and the teams around you to routinely outperform expectations.

EXAMPLES OF POWERFUL BRAND PROMISES

Here are some of the finest examples of brand promises ever recorded. Some of these firms would be expected to make a list, while others may come as a surprise, but it demonstrates that a great brand is composed of much more than a logo, icon, or a catchy slogan.

1) McDonald's: "Simple, effortless pleasure."

McDonald's has clearly outlined what its consumers may anticipate from their interactions with the company. They have kept it basic without overpromising to guarantee that the promise is preserved and consistently fulfilled. Not only do they have a clearly defined promise, but they also have an unrivaled commitment to upholding that promise.

. . .

2) Coca-Cola: "To inspire moments of optimism and uplift."

Coca-Cola's brand promise is quite unconventional. The mission statement does not reference the company's products or services; rather, it tries to reflect the company's employees' shared philosophy. Coca-Cola portrays itself as a lifestyle brand that is about much more than just producing successful beverages with this brand promise.

3) Nike's: "To inspire and innovate for every athlete* in the globe."

Nike, like Coca-Cola, does not name their products but instead emphasizes its benefits. Through their products and services, Nike achieves the feeling of inspiration and innovation that they seek to convey. If a person has a body, they are an athlete, as indicated by the asterisk next to the word. This makes Nike a brand of the general public as opposed to the athletes who promote the brand.

4) BMW: "The Ultimate Driving Machine"

This audacious assertion is the driving force behind the BMW brand. Their brand promise asserts confidently that they intend to manufacture only the most efficient and stylish vehicles.

5) Apple: "Think different."

Apple as a brand spares no effort when it comes to giving precise services. Whether it's in the shape of luxury products or the apple support network, apple's offerings extend beyond its marketing methods and product sales. Apple excels in every category. The brand pledges to fulfill the objective of giving customers the dedication to think creatively and innovate their ideas. In addition, they encourage customers to do the same and not follow the crowd.

6) H&M: "More fashion choices that are good for people, the planet, and your wallet."

Options that are both economical and environmentally beneficial! H&m is able to express its mission through their brand promise in a concise manner that catches the customers' attention. They will be supplied with fashionable options that are kind to the environment and their wallets.

7) Starbucks' mission statement is: "To inspire and nurture the human spirit, one person, one cup, and one neighborhood at a time."

With a fan base as recognizable as Apple's, it's hardly surprising that Starbucks is a superb example of a brand that consistently delivers on its promise. Starbucks, like many other companies, has defined itself as a lifestyle brand seeking to deliver the world much more than a fantastic cup of coffee.

8) Walmart: "Save money, live better."

Walmart's brand promise of saving money and ultimately living a better life persuaded its customers with relative ease. Low costs on essentials are already an excellent method of brand promotion. Walmart takes a step further by tying the emotional advantage of having a better life to its low costs. This strengthens the relationship with clients.

. . .

9) Coors Light: "The World's Most Refreshing Beer."

This straightforward brand promise is both straightforward and instructive, expressing the essence of the business in a single statement. While "refreshing" may imply different things to different individuals, the concept of a light beer as a whole is generally acknowledged, and a degree of exaggeration is implied (and accepted) by the claim "world's most."

10) Harley Davidson: "We are Harley Davidson."

Over time, the brand promises of Harley Davidson have evolved. All of them, though, have just concluded that there is nothing like Harley. The breakthrough brand requires no complex brand promise. They are aware that people are familiar with the brand. Therefore, the latest brand promise retains the familiarity and ensures that the organization gives a constant and coherent experience.

HOW TO KEEP THE PROMISES OF YOUR BRAND?

According to the adage, actions speak louder than words. When it comes to delivering on brand commitments to customers, this proverb holds true. Developing a powerful brand requires more than a bright logo or memorable tagline. It is a promise and a commitment made to your customers. Maintaining the brand promise creates brand equity with future customers and also engages current customers, who are the most valuable customers you can acquire. Successful organizations uphold these assurances and guarantee that outstanding service is continually provided throughout the client journey. If promises are not kept, they have no value.

. . .

1) Remain constant

Obviously, the difficulty is actually doing it. Be inventive, not creative. Introducing an entirely new product or service during a moment of crisis may lead to customer confusion and personnel burnout. Now is the time for the majority of firms to remain in their comfort zone and focus on continuously delivering on the promises they have previously made to their customers, modified to their current circumstances. Maintaining your brand's promise is one of the most critical things you can do to demonstrate that you value your customers, regardless of any potential disruptions.

2) Solicit feedback

Businesses can run surveys to gauge the brand's resonance with customers and staff. Do customers consider it appealing, unusual, and believable? Based on their recent experiences, do customers believe that the organization is delivering on its promises? Do the employees comprehend it? How committed are they? The responses to these questions can help businesses make improvements to better effectively deliver their brand promises.

3) Train your employees efficiently

Since your employees are the first point of contact between your clients and your company, it is imperative that they leave a positive and lasting impression. Staff training is essential to guaranteeing the fulfillment of brand commitments. The attitude and actions of your customer care crew will be a deciding factor for customers, as they will demonstrate how much your company values them. Therefore, it is essential that your support employees be armed with the relevant information, honed in soft skills, and taught your business's vision. Make your staff a part of the brand evolution by involving them in every business choice you make so that you may receive various inputs. Prepare and record your action plan to provide greater clarity to your personnel and assist them in making the best decisions.

4) Monitor performance

It is essential for businesses to measure how well they deliver on their promises and to establish standards for evaluating performance via regularly scheduled evaluations. Consider a corporation whose brand promise incorporates customer responsiveness. To promote this objective, the company establishes a policy requiring a response to every written customer request within 48 hours and to every phone conversation within five minutes. To ensure compliance with these standards, the organization can require meticulous record-keeping and the logging of enquiries and complaints. Monitoring, developing early threat identification, and efficient risk management can assist firms in transforming potential risks into opportunities to advance their strategic objectives.

5) Hit every touchpoint

A customer's experience encompasses more than conversing with a sales representative or an onboarding expert. It consists of all client touch-points and interactions, including social media, your website, and your product. Your customer promise is the foundation of every customer touchpoint and contact, including your online user experience and the attitudes of your customer care personnel. If you claim to sell eco-friendly items, does your packaging reflect this claim? If you claim to offer hassle-free service, is your website quick and simple to navigate?

Every touchpoint must fulfill your promise. Examine the whole customer journey, from discovery to post-sale, and consider how your brand may execute its customer promise more effectively. Customers' satisfaction is vital to the success of enterprises. Create a customer promise and commit to keeping it if you want your customers to feel positive about your brand.

IMPORTANCE OF KEEPING YOUR BRAND PROMISE

Unlike previous generations, today's consumers have an overwhelming number of options in every area, from hundreds of shoe brands to a seemingly endless list of cell phone service providers. Therefore, brands have had to find a means to differentiate themselves in order to remain memorable in consumers' thoughts.

Usually, the greatest approach to stand out is to stand for something. This "something" is a promise, not a slogan or marketing gimmick. What distinguishes great brands from the rest of the competition is the contract they create with their customers — a promise to give something consistent throughout every encounter and aspect of their business.

1) It tells individuals what to anticipate from your brand

The common belief is that without anticipation, there is no disappointment. People will be dissatisfied if they don't receive exactly what you've promised when they connect with your business if they're aware of the benefits you've promised.

. . .

2) A brand promise clarifies your organization's objectives concisely

Although your phrase may be memorable, your brand promise is significant. The key to success is effectively communicating the value of your brand, and your brand promise must encompass every area of your business. Regardless of how complicated your business is, your brand promise must make it accessible to everyone.

3) Which promises should you make to your customers?

When individuals and businesses fail to deliver on their brand promises, they are unable to build or retain differentiation within their respective brand categories. This indicates that your customers lack brand loyalty. That means they are equally likely to purchase an alternative widget over yours. In the opposite case, when a corporation exceeds expectations, it is possible to foster a sense of community and family. The optimal customer experience generates the type of clients you desire: those that generate additional revenue. You want them to feel committed to your organization. When you marry someone, you expect that person to remain monogamous, and you want consumers to feel the same way about your brand.

4) A brand promise creates a meaningful connection

Creating a direct connection with your target audience is a vital component of delivering a brand promise. People who will become lifelong consumers will not only be admirers of your goods but also believers in what you stand for. However, if you do not present this in black and white (or fully animated color video), you will miss an opportunity to bring new individuals into your brand's universe. Deepening your relationships with your consumers may seem like a big endeavor, but the truth is that you've probably already been doing it simply by speaking with them in person over the phone. This relationship finally enables you to comprehend what is vital to your clients, why those things are significant to them, and how your organization fits their demands.

Once you comprehend this, you may begin to apply this understanding to your interactions with them. Not only will you discover that the beliefs of your current customers correspond with yours, but you will also begin to attract more individuals who share your values, thereby strengthening their trust and expanding your brand's reach.

5) Sets you apart from your competitors

With a distinct, truthful, and memorable brand promise, your clients will be able to identify your brand, its offers, and features that set you apart from other companies providing comparable or identical services. Your brand promise emphasizes the distinctive benefits prospects will receive from your brand that is unavailable elsewhere.

There is a prevalent social phenomenon known as "what you ordered versus what you got." This simply indicates that a customer chose to do business with you based on your public image. However, they receive something incredibly disheartening when the things arrive. The thing just does not meet the initial expectations you had for it. No one needs to inform you that you will not receive such a customer in the future.

6) Pursuing and receiving feedback

You may be enjoying success as a result of your diligence, aspirations, and selling talents. Your product's abundance of features can also be a factor in obtaining high sales volume. However, there is one important factor that will significantly increase your sales: "Follow-ups." Sales follow-up is essential for establishing and maintaining long-term relationships. It entails a straightforward communication attempt to evaluate consumer interest, comprehends their challenges, and determine their fundamental needs for which they may be seeking a solution.

HOW TO FOLLOW UP ON YOUR CUSTOMERS?

Many businesses are concerned with attracting customers, but they don't always consider what happens to them once they've made a purchase. Excellent customer service continues beyond the point of transaction. Existing clients must be followed up with if you wish to establish a long-lasting relationship with your customers.

1) Determine the prospect's interest

Understanding your prospects' interests is a never-ending adventure, but obtaining insight and a better understanding of consumers and consumer behavior is necessary to stay on top of your industry and competition. Sales representatives are continually looking for novel methods to forecast the behavior of their target buyers. Start by segmenting your potential consumers depending on who is talking about your business, who is following or connecting with you, and who has faith in your products and demonstrates purchasing intent. Once the audience has been categorized, determine what topics they are interested in. By doing so, you can gain fantastic insights into your prospects, which can assist your sales staff in making important business decisions.

. . .

2) Sales follow up email

70 percent of consumers make a purchase choice around
five times after initial contact, according to research (Marcel
Schwantes, 2022). In sales, repetition is essential. Occasionally,
though, we become so wary of pursuing individuals that we
send them tedious and unsolicited emails with material such as
"just checking in." There is a fine line between sending an effective, helpful sales follow-up email and becoming obnoxious.
The objective of sales follow-up should be to provide consistent
value and keep prospects progressing through the purchase
cycle. This is also known as relevant lead nurturing. Informative
guides, video lessons, and reports that enhance your prospects'
buying experiences should be provided to them throughout the
buying cycle.

3) Create a directory of prospects

You cannot effectively advertise your brand unless you
know who you want to promote. Creating a prospecting directory involves finding the ideal clients for your specific services.
Creating a directory of prospects is one of the most effective
techniques to avoid becoming overwhelmed and maintain
focus on end objectives. When working from a prospecting
directory, marketing efforts and business management become
more structured. Your prospect directory need not be elaborate;
a simple spreadsheet that keeps your ideas and thoughts
collected in one location will suffice.

The sales follow-up call is a crucial component of the sales
cycle. A sales follow-up call is more difficult than a cold call the
ability to create a relationship with the prospect. You might
investigate further by asking pertinent questions to learn about

their concerns and comprehend the scenario. Be sincerely interested in assisting them. If you are unable to seal the purchase, you will at least have a more robust information base to better service additional prospects throughout the buying cycle.

5) Evaluate the sales lifecycle in order to determine the efficacy of your communication

High-quality customer interactions comprise a high-quality customer experience. Any business that wishes to use the customer experience as a competitive advantage should prioritize eliciting a positive response at every touchpoint. Attempting to assess client experiences with a single statistic is frequently an inefficient and excessively simplified strategy. Measuring and managing a portfolio of metrics that includes touchpoint data can provide invaluable insight into what is and is not working.

THE SIGNIFICANCE OF FOLLOWING UP WITH YOUR CUSTOMERS

This implies that the frequency of your touch with prospects will impact how quickly they make a purchase. Constant communication enables you to better comprehend your clients' needs and devise strategies to assist them in realizing them. Regular follow-up gives clients the opportunity to be heard and effectively engaged. Additionally, consistent communication helps customers remember you when they have a need that you can meet.

Prospects may be preoccupied, require time to consider the product or service being offered, or simply have no immediate need for your goods. This is why, as a sales executive, you should never accept "No" as the final conclusion. You have no way of knowing why a prospect did not respond, and the only way to discover the reason is to follow up.

If your clients feel as though you've forgotten about them after you've sold them something, they are less inclined to purchase from you again. If you fail to deliver excellent customer service and follow-up, your customers may feel tricked since it may appear that you were only trying to make a quick sale.

2) Customer follow-up raises the likelihood of repeat business

Which company is more likely to retain a customer? One that contacts it's clients or one that disregards them? The solution is obvious. By following up, you afford yourself the opportunity to rectify any errors that may have occurred during your connection with the consumer. The input you receive will not only assist you in salvaging a single customer connection but also in enhancing your customer service routine as a whole.

3) Customer experience

Following up with customers enhances their overall impression of your business. You may even resolve issues before they become a problem. For instance, if you continue to connect with your clients after a sale has been made, you will be able to promptly resolve any issues they had with your items. If you demonstrate to your clients that you are willing to assist them and prevent problems before they arise, you will avoid unfavorable internet reviews, and you may even save your firm a significant number of refunds.

· · ·

4) Following up with clients gives you a competitive advantage

Do all businesses contact customers after they've completed a purchase? Not likely. You will immediately surpass your opponents or, at the very least, avoid falling behind. Assuming other companies are following up with their consumers and your company isn't, you're unlikely to win the hearts of the members of your target audience.

5) Feedback

There is a good likelihood that by following up with clients, you can increase your overall customer feedback. If you follow up with your consumers to ensure they are satisfied with your services, you will boost your likelihood of receiving positive feedback. Consider that a positive experience may drive your present clients to inform others about your business. Word-of-mouth advertising is quite effective; if a customer loves your company and the way you handled their sale, there's a strong chance they'll tell a friend or family member who is seeking similar services.

IMPORTANCE OF HAVING EXCELLENT CUSTOMER SUPPORT

Customer support is a subset of customer service that prioritizes consumers who are experiencing difficulties or need assistance with a purchased product or service. Customer support teams give technical assistance with products and answer inquiries regarding purchases and experiences. The objective of customer support teams is for consumers to leave engagements with answers, solutions, and happy experiences. Customer support encompasses tasks such as responding to customer inquiries, assisting with onboarding, resolving issues, and upgrading clients to a new product or service.

Customer support typically refers to teams in SaaS and tech organizations tasked with aiding customers with goods and services requiring ongoing tech support. Customer service representatives should have an in-depth understanding of the company's products and services. Their responsibilities may also include writing articles for the customer care center.

1) Customers will remember this

People will never forget whether your customer support was exceptional or bad. You really do not want them to recall the latter. You may question why people recall customer support so vividly, but the answer should be rather obvious: because your customers interact with you actively. Not only are they viewing your items, but they are also interacting with a representative of your organization.

2) Representation of brand image

Your brand's image, goal, and vision, as well as what and who you represent, are always communicated to the owner and the staff. As a business owner, you are aware of what you typically deliver and accomplish, as are your staff. However, for your customers and the wider public, the customer support team is responsible for portraying your brand and what it stands for.

3) It reflects heavily on your entire organization

Everything associated with your business reflects on everything else. People will presume your products are of high quality if you provide excellent customer service. People will assume your things are subpar if your customer service is subpar. The same applies in reverse for shipping, refunds, services, and any other circumstance. Even if this is not exactly accurate, you must recognize that this is how your customers believe.

4) Competitive advantage

One of the most important aspects of customer service is the competitive edge it provides over competing brands. Regardless of the business or area in which you operate, there will inevitably be competitors offering the same products and services as you. To distinguish yourself, you must prioritize your consumers and make them feel appreciated.

5) It's an excellent marketing angle

From a purely business perspective, excellent customer service is an excellent marketing angle. It's something you may highlight in your advertising, which is certain to attract more customers. People appreciate hearing that you provide exceptional customer service, plain and simple. Anything that can improve your marketing effectiveness is worth the extra effort. This viewpoint is most effective when other real customers are praising your customer service, so feel free to solicit reviews and testimonials.

WHY THE CUSTOMER IS ALWAYS RIGHT? (IDEA BEHIND THIS AND WHY THIS MINDSET IS GREAT)

The customer is always right is an aphorism, which is a brief proverb that can be used to convey an idea concisely. The statement that the customer is always right cannot be termed a proverb because it is not a universally accepted truth.

The customer is always right implies that the client's interests and aspirations are always important. The inference is that customer service and customer satisfaction are the most important objectives, regardless of whether or not the customer is in the wrong. Marshall Field, who opened a renowned department store in Chicago, Illinois, in 1852, created the expression "the customer is always right." The customer is always right is a catchphrase that emerged during the turn of the twentieth century. H. Gordon Selfridge, who formerly worked for Field and later founded a department store in England, brought the slogan with him. Interestingly, about the same period, the Frenchman César Ritz coined the expression "the customer is always right" Obviously, the customer is frequently incorrect in his expectations and attributions of responsibility. However, the popular phrase "the customer is always right" is still frequently used to encourage shops to prioritize customer pleasure over other objectives.

WHY IS THE BUYER ALWAYS RIGHT?

You likely look forward to launching your business. This is conceivable, but you should be aware that the decision should be taken after considering client feedback. Yes, "customers are business," and they have an equal voice with the owner. In actuality, customers dominate the business sector, not the owner. The success or failure of your customers depends on your customers. Always guarantee that you provide excellent customer service to your clients unless you want to see your business fail.

Businesses who consider their customers as royalty, the most valuable asset in the company, have recorded higher returns than their competitors, who place minimal importance on customers. There is no business known that can function without customers. Any action taken by a corporation is intended to impress its clients.

1) Customers are the foundation of your business

Your primary clients constitute your business. Without them and their commitment, you might be forced to close your office within days. Their feedback and complaints should be your company's first priority. In any case, if you do not do so, a competitor will. And it is not ideal for a competitor to steal away your main customer base. Ensure that you're adopting many tactics that enable you to resolve and accommodate client comments and concerns more quickly and efficiently.

2) Customer retention

It is not simple to acquire and retain the same customers! It takes considerable effort to recruit customers to your business, and losing them is the last thing on your mind. Once you have acquired clients, you should shift your attention to retaining them rather than acquiring new ones.

In many instances, existing clients are neglected in favor of acquiring new ones. And the majority of the time, they wind up losing twice. Not acquiring new customers and losing old ones. Always remember that your customer is your boss, and provide them with the greatest service possible. Most key, cultivate customer communication. This is certain to keep them around.

3) Customer backlash is real and can be detrimental to your company

If you disregard your core customers' input for too long, they may turn against you in the worst-case situation. And customer resentment can be costly and time-consuming to remedy. Consider Apple Maps, New Coke, Netflix's shelved Qwikster spin-off, as well as numerous more products that did not meet the expectations of the company's primary audience.

Was their feedback considered in the creation of these products? Probably not as much as they ought to have. This costly error has already been made by several companies around the world; therefore, there is no need for you to repeat it.

4) Customers are the business

A business is created to fulfill the demands of certain individuals. Customers constitute a company's market. This demonstrates why businesses cannot exist without consumers! Customers are necessary for the success of your firm. Always ask yourself this question when developing a company plan: who are your target customers? This assists you in putting everything in place to guarantee they receive the best service possible.

5) It can help you uncover new revenue streams

Similar to how consumer feedback and complaints can help alleviate customer pain points. Additionally, they can assist you in identifying fresh chances for new product lines and revenue streams.

REASONS WHY THE CUSTOMER ISN'T ALWAYS RIGHT

In a literal sense, customers are not always correct. Occasionally, they are jerks or in a terrible mood. Sometimes they commit errors and place the blame on your personnel. That does not imply you should respond in kind. As a result, it is not always appropriate for a leader to take the customer's side.

You should support your employees if, for instance, a customer is being obviously impolite. If not, no one will want to work for you. There are more reasons why the consumer is not always correct. The following section will explain why the customer is not always right.

1) It Causes Excessive Stress for Employees

Regardless of your clientele, you will certainly encounter at least a few unreasonable and hostile customers. Numerous examples exist of personnel giving inadequate customer service. Know how to distinguish this from an unreasonable customer. Try your best to mediate the disagreement, but if you must pick between siding with the customer or your employee, it is advisable to choose the employee's side. In the long term, supporting your staff will always benefit your firm. Happy personnel will go over and above to give excellent service and satisfy your clients.

2) Some clients are just detrimental to a business's value

Unfavorable customers can reduce the worth of a company. If you attend a sporting event and become disruptive, for instance, you will be ejected. Even though you are a paying customer, you may not interfere with the experience of others.

In addition, your interference diminishes the value of the sporting event itself. Customers will not attend an event if they learn that the staff will tolerate unruly individuals.

3) It strains the management-employee relationship

If a business owner frequently sides with the customer in times of disagreement without allowing the employee to have input, it demoralizes the employee and can lead to ill will. Frequently, the employee resents management and becomes bitter. This can cause a very negative impact on their job performance, resulting in inferior customer service to other clients.

4) Certain customers are simply in error

There are those people in life to whom you must stand up. In business, it is the same. Your business cannot tolerate customers who are threatening, unruly, or disrespectful. If you permit such conduct, you will face blowback from other customers, staff, or both. In addition to the moral need to do so, it is also smart business to confront consumers who behave inappropriately. In addition, you should empower personnel to address incorrect clients. In this approach, your employees can establish a safe and polite environment for everyone.

5) Your reserves are not endless

If the customer is always right, no organization has sufficient resources to resolve every problem. Because you would require a limitless amount of resources, there is a reason why policies are formed, so create them and adhere to them. The policy serves as an agreement between you and your consumers for conducting business. Recognize that you cannot handle everything so that you do not allow clients to deplete your resources.

WHAT IS BUSINESS SUSTAINABILITY ALL ABOUT?

Sustainability in business, also referred to as corporate sustainability, is the management and synchronization of environmental, social, and financial demands and concerns to ensure continued, responsible, and ethical success. Going "green" is much more than a passing fad for many firms. It is part of a strategy to improve the business's sustainability, which entails minimizing negative environmental and social impacts and ensuring that future generations have sufficient resources to meet their demands.

Not only are sustainable businesses good stewards of the environment, but they are also well-positioned to compete in the global economy. Investors, consumers, and even job-seekers consider a company's social and environmental reputation. Businesses that do not implement sustainable practices run the danger of losing a portion of their target market. The media contributes significantly to the sustainability movement by informing us of business practices that hurt persons and the environment.

Sustainability is becoming increasingly important for all industries and enterprises. Most leaders now believe that a sustainability plan is essential. Multiple factors are "kept at a certain level": the environment, yes, but also the larger society, both monetarily and in terms of social justice. There are various official definitions of sustainability in business, but they all boil down to the premise that you may establish a more lucrative corporation by considering the impact of your organization's operations on the environment and society as a whole.

WHY IS SUSTAINABILITY IMPORTANT IN BUSINESS?

The economic case for sustainability is unmistakable. It will assist you in innovating, expanding your client base, reducing expenses, assessing risk, maximizing opportunities, and recruiting and retaining the best staff.

There are a number of reasons why sustainable business practices are crucial. And some of them are entirely altruistic: organizations have considerable potential to cause change, from their impact on the environment to the introduction and standardization of eco-friendly practices to D&I initiatives that contribute to an equal society over time. Alternatively said, having a sustainable firm has many environmental and social benefits. However, this offers benefits for the firm itself.

1) Enhances brand image and gives firms a competitive advantage

The most prosperous businesses are those that are able to overcome competition. Due to the fact that many business owners already compete for the same customer base, only those who distinguish themselves can grow and expand sustainably. One of the simplest ways to keep clients coming back is to ensure that your offer is superior to those of your competitors. Ensure that your brand's presentation is attractive to potential clients and purchasers. Although advertising is effective, it is easier to generate results when clients know they can rely on your items to provide the greatest deals. For instance, it is advantageous for a business to comprehend what makes its clients joyful. Some clients will only purchase products or visit your institution if you adhere to environmental regulations.

· · ·

2) Contribute to the preservation of the environment

Protecting the environment and the health of local communities is the first and most obvious benefit of being a green business. An organization that is sustainable is carbon neutral or climate positive. This means having a little or no negative impact on the environment, balancing any CO_2 released into the atmosphere with an equal quantity removed, or a positive impact, exceeding net-zero by removing additional CO_2 from the atmosphere. Sustainable practices enable organizations to cut waste, reduce carbon risk, and enhance energy efficiency.

3) Minimizes costs and boosts productivity

Whether your office is physically present or you're considering hiring the best virtual office in London, your overall objective should be to ensure the sustainability of your organization. The company will reach a point where profits flow smoothly, which is one of the key benefits of an eco-friendly business. Once an industry achieves profitability, it continues to grow and flourish without requiring additional resources.

4) Enhance company capability and resiliency

Sustainability enhances corporate resiliency and facilitates compliance with regulations, hence enabling the avoidance of green penalties through sustainable practices. Conferences such as the COP 26 UN Climate Change Conference, convened by the United Nations Framework Convention on Climate Change (UNFCCC), demonstrate the importance of change, prompting additional dialogue and greener legislation that affects and will continue to affect corporate practices.

When organizations engage in sustainable manufacturing processes, the likelihood of wasting resources is also dimin-

ished. One of the most secure corporate practices would be
recycling, which ensures that all resources are utilized effectively. Fortunately, this is a simple task, as all business owners
need to identify areas where recycling may be integrated into
their systems and processes.

WHAT IS INNOVATION IN BUSINESS ALL ABOUT?

Innovation is essential to your company's success in today's
very competitive business environment, particularly as
customers become more discerning and demanding. Entrepreneurs need a competitive advantage to thrive and stand out.
Innovation can create a competitive advantage, thereby
enhancing production, growth, and profitability. Innovation is,
at its most fundamental level, coming up with a new way to do
things. When it comes to business innovation, new ways of
doing things are implemented with the intention of generating
more revenue. Beyond this description, corporate innovation is
a broad notion applicable to a variety of products, services,
initiatives, and regulations. It may include new items that will
better serve customers or a new program that will improve staff
communication regarding ongoing projects.

To achieve competitive advantages, a firm or organization
must be able to adapt and innovate in response to shifting
trends and new generations. Innovations apply to all levels and
sizes of management and organizations in all industries. Innovations generate greater prospects and are essential to a
company's survival, economic growth, and success. Innovation
facilitates the creation of novel ideas and is a catalyst for opti-
mizing processes. Innovative businesses are able to shift their
organizational paradigm in order to uncover new opportunities
and the most effective solutions to current problems.

In order to achieve innovation, leaders must be receptive

and cooperative. To innovate, it is necessary to be at ease with uncertainty and to successfully manage change. Innovative leaders are inquisitive and hopeful because they are willing to take chances. Nobody can predict where innovation will lead a business or an individual.

IMPORTANCE OF INNOVATION IN BUSINESS

Change is accelerating so rapidly that innovation has become an urgent strategic and structural requirement. It is the key competitive lever left to secure both the survival and sustainability of an organization. Living in the Disruption, Digitization, and Connection Ages, we must focus on strengthening adaptability, creativity, and ingenuity while also investigating what it means to be human. In addition to strengthening our capacity to generate customer empathy and a customer-centric focus.

If an organization is not advancing, it cannot maintain its relevance. Organizations frequently collaborate with other organizations. Therefore, it is sometimes difficult to comprehend the effects of innovation. Innovation encompasses much more than companies seeking a competitive advantage. Innovation is the driving force behind modern existence. Here are five tangible advantages that innovation can provide to your business.

1) Innovation assists businesses in differentiating themselves

Innovation is fundamentally about doing something differently than everyone else in your industry. If your firm uses innovation on its products, for instance, the objective is to develop or update the products until there is nothing else on the market that is comparable. If your firm is applying innovation to its processes, it is because doing so will save you time, money, or other resources and provide you with a competitive advantage over companies whose processes have not evolved. In either case, your firm is attempting something new because remaining with the status quo is ineffective. It would be a huge error to miss a further major benefit: innovation helps a company differentiate itself and its products from the competitors, which may be especially effective in a saturated industry or market.

Without adaptability, you may be restricting your company's progress. Firms with adequate resources may be able to acquire competitors and develop in this manner, but the growth of the majority of businesses will be constrained by their ability to innovate and find new ways to attract customers and expand their market share.

3) Enhance sales and client interactions

If you fail to enhance your products and services, you risk losing clients to more innovative rivals. If you invest time and resources in innovation, your customers will recognize and value the added value you're providing. This should result in increased sales. You can begin with modest activities such as conducting frequent consumer surveys to identify potential product enhancements and establishing an innovation team to lead your efforts.

2) Better growth

The digital age has introduced an era of extraordinary growth and transformation. Ninety percent of the world's data was created in the last few years, and hundreds of new websites are established every minute. Those who cannot keep up with the changes will undoubtedly be left behind in this atmosphere of constant change.

5) Boost your market position

Innovation can help you predict market shifts and possibilities more rapidly, allowing you to avoid being compelled to respond to adjustments. Additionally, it can assist you in standing out from the competition. This innovation can be generated by regularly evaluating market trends, listening to consumers, suppliers, and advisers, and understanding what competitors are doing in order to identify opportunities and seize them.

6

REPEATING THROUGH LOYALTY

Most consumers have a propensity to purchase products or services from a firm they have previously purchased from and are familiar with. Whether we recognize it or not, we are all loyal to particular brands. And this brand loyalty significantly impacts our purchase decisions. When a customer is brand loyal, they feel more at ease purchasing from that brand than from its competitors. This is the foundation of a strong customer-brand relationship; therefore, if you want to learn how to profit from brand loyalty, you must familiarize yourself with it.

Typically, companies with an established brand name operate in a highly competitive market where both old and new rival items exist. Typically, many techniques are employed by businesses to establish and sustain brand loyalty. For example, the marketing department may closely monitor consumer purchasing patterns. This is done in order to develop relationships with their clients through customer service. Typically, for a brand loyalty campaign to be deemed successful, it must meet essential market segment characteristics.

WHAT IS BRAND LOYALTY?

Brand loyalty refers to the specific bond a consumer has to a particular product. This is demonstrated by the customers' continued purchases of a certain product despite the availability of alternatives. In other words, brand loyalty occurs when a buyer regularly purchases a product from a single producer, excluding brands from other providers. Businesses benefit from brand loyalty because recurring purchases produce increased revenues and customer referrals.

Brand loyalty is the propensity for consumers to consistently choose one brand over another. Consumer behavior patterns indicate that consumers will continue to purchase products from a company with which they have established a relationship of trust. Businesses benefit greatly from client loyalty since it leads to repeat purchases, increased income, and customer referrals.

Some brands utilize brand loyalty equations to calculate the level of consumer or total brand loyalty they enjoy. This can be a combination of customer lifetime value, customer churn, the share of wallet, or other metrics deemed relevant by the brand. Companies will leverage brand loyalty to increase sales of existing items as well as those of related products and brands.

WHYS IS BRAND LOYALTY IMPORTANT?

A devoted customer base can help a firm surpass its competition and offer it the necessary competitive edge to prosper in the market. Customers with strong brand loyalty will continue to purchase a company's products or services regardless of price or convenience changes. A powerful brand supported by a devoted consumer base can endure any micro-or macro environmental condition. Whether there is a macroeconomic reces-

sion or a microlevel company reorganization, brand devotees
will continue to purchase the brands they adore.

Note that aside from the repeated purchase of a product
from a single vendor, loyalty may also be proven by actions
such as word-of-mouth promotion. This is where you describe
how great a product is and why others should continue using it
rather than switching to a different brand. There is also brand
loyalty when people are willing to pay a premium price for a
particular good despite the availability of cheaper competitors.

1) It creates obstacles for new rivals to enter the market

You have greater protection against market share loss since
new competitors are less likely to enter a market characterized
by intense brand loyalty. Imagine attempting to unseat Amazon
as the most popular online store or Google as the most popular
search engine. Not impossible, but certainly a hard assignment

Here, it is crucial to caution incumbent businesses not to
take brand loyalty for granted; it should never be assumed.
Numerous once-powerful firms have succumbed to competition because they assumed their market position, and positive
client sentiments would endure forever.

2) Establishes credibility

You can thrive by establishing credibility with your
consumers. Did you know that eighty percent of consumers cite
trust as a factor in their shopping decisions? (Peep Laja, 2019)
Seventy-six percent of customers responded that for them to be
loyal to a brand, they must believe that if they suggest the
company to a friend, that friend will likewise have a positive
experience.

. . .

3) Existing consumers are less expensive to acquire than new ones

Acquiring new customers is more expensive. They may also be more demanding, requiring helplines and attention because, first, they do not know the firm as well and, second, they need to be handled well while comparison shopping. If you do not provide them with excellent service, they will go somewhere. This is true of all customers, but it is especially true of new clients who have not yet invested in your business. If you can retain clients and maintain their loyalty, your customer service costs should decrease.

4) It creates an emotional bond

Loyalty creates emotional bonds since it allows you to demonstrate your alignment with the customer. The majority of customers are driven to demonstrate stronger brand loyalty if the brand shares their values.

5) Brand champions

Loyal customers can help your business in ways outside of using their credit cards. Whether you refer to them as brand champions, Net Promoters, or word-of-mouth marketing heroes, all of your satisfied consumers have the ability to bring you additional business. This could be done via social media, reviews, or word of mouth.

BUILDING BRAND LOYALTY

Customers who are devoted to a particular brand do not purchase an alternative brand when the favored brand is unavailable. Instead, people prefer to search multiple stores for their favorite brand. In the event that they cannot locate it, they will defer the purchase until the stores are supplied with it. Note that a consumer's purchasing decision can be either conscious or unconscious. Nonetheless, it is greatly dependent on the level of consumer trust achieved by the brand. Customers' beliefs and attitudes are what constitutes a brand. Always consumers want a brand to fulfill their emotional or physical requirements in a distinctive manner.

There are a few things your organization must do well in order to earn clients' trust and keep them coming back.

1) Provide excellent quality and value

One of the most obvious strategies to establish brand loyalty is to fulfill all of your promises to the highest possible standard. Never disappointing them. Your services and goods must be of the highest quality, and you must maintain this standard in all you do so that the value you provide is never questioned. Determine what satisfies your customers and concentrate your efforts there. If you are able to exceed the client's expectations, there will be no reason for the client to consider your competition.

2) An accurate comprehension of the consumer journey

Historically, businesses have assessed their performance based on sales. But as our understanding of customer experience evolves, we can see that each purchase is part of a wider picture — the customer journey. This includes your marketing and customer-focused advertising, your retail experience (online or offline), reviews of your products and those of your competitors, and what happens after a customer receives your product or service. Collectively, these touch-points impact client loyalty, and by examining the entire journey, you can concentrate your efforts where they will have the greatest impact.

3) Know your customer

If you do not know your audience, you cannot develop trust and loyalty. Understanding more about the clients you serve every day is essential to the success of your organization. Only if you understand the requirements and goals of your end consumer will you be able to target your efforts effectively and convert him into a true fan of your items. Knowing your audience enables you to control the behavior and reactions of your clients through the use of specific triggers.

4) Tell your brand's story

The brand's story should elicit the client's empathy. A compelling brand story helps you distinguish out from the competition by highlighting your company's distinct approach or history. This is something your regular consumers will talk about with their coworkers during a coffee break while showing them what they've purchased from your store. This is what drives the audience's interest.

5) Acquire social proof

Social proof for your brand may be attained through a variety of social networks. You can collaborate with influencers and celebrities or target a certain niche with a strong partnership with another business in the same area.

THE DISTINCTION BETWEEN CONSUMER AND BRAND LOYALTY

Clearly, there is a close relationship between these two concepts, as brand loyalty is frequently associated with being a loyal customer of a particular brand. But, there are a few distinctions between these two:

Customer loyalty is frequently assessed by how frequently a customer makes purchases, how much they spend, and how active and engaged they are with your brand. A devoted customer speaks positively about you and promotes you to others.

Brand loyalty has absolutely nothing to do with money or expenditures. It is all about the way your customers perceive your brand. A consumer who has made only one or two purchases from your company can nonetheless be extremely devoted to your brand. They are utterly enamored with the brand's experience and the way your products make them feel when they use or wear them.

REWARDING BRAND LOYALTY

Brand loyalty is the possibility that a customer will do business with you again. This is a result of consumer happiness and is more important than availability, pricing, and other factors that generally influence purchasing decisions. When a customer is loyal to a product, service, or brand, they are willing to wait for restocking or pay a small premium.

One of the most effective strategies to retain clients is to reward their loyalty. Customers who remain loyal to your business are the driving force behind your success. In fact, loyal consumers spend 67 percent more than one-time customers, which is why it is essential to prioritize repeat business. How, then?

1) Form alliances with other organizations to provide more inclusive services

Similarly, if you can provide additional incentives for being your customer, you will move even further down the spectrum of brand loyalty. Are you able to collaborate with similar organizations to provide your customers with additional benefits, such as discounted memberships or free food and drink? Consider what your clients would like in this regard — what they value - and devise a discount program that satisfies this demand. Regardless of the size of your organization, strategic relationships should not be disregarded, and you should seek out similar/local organizations to collaborate with.

2) Host a preview event

Formulate an event around a new product, a new service offering, or even a software update, and allow your top customers to preview it and have the first opportunity to order it. You want this event to feel exclusive and special, so ensure that the ambiance and refreshments are elegant and that customers have adequate time and space to socialize with one another, with you and your employees, and to learn about the new product.

3) Create a community for your customers

We all enjoy feeling a part of communities that provide mutual benefits, such as possibilities for personal development and social connection. Digital communities, such as LinkedIn/Facebook Groups and Forums, are a good starting point, but you may also develop real events and communities where your consumers can congregate and debate issues of their choosing. Customers will always place more faith in their peers than in your organization. Create an atmosphere in which your consumers can participate that they would not be able to if they were not your clients.

4) Compose a thank-you note

Yes, a real, handwritten note on a beautiful card that cites previous purchases and the name of the customer's business. Writing a customized, personalized message to a wonderful customer is a significant approach to expressing your gratitude because handwritten notes are so rare that they are now considered special.

5) Honor the client

Although your customer helps pay your organization's bills, he or she is a real person and real people like being recognized for their efforts. Can you celebrate the client or organization in any way to express your gratitude and make them feel valued? Using owned channels, you can include stories or snippets about your customers and the role they play in your business. This acknowledgement could go a long way toward persuading other consumers who are admirers of your company to contribute more to your success.

7
IF EVERYTHING IS DONE CORRECTLY, HOW IT WILL SELL ITSELF?

I t is one thing to have content customers. It is something else entirely to have satisfied consumers who remember you the next time they make a purchase. And still, another is to have clients who promote you to their friends. And it's another else entirely to have consumers who adore your product or service so much that they become product evangelists and can't wait for the chance to rave about how awesome it is. The advocacy or community phase of your business is significant from two angles. This stage provides the opportunity to foster a sense of community among prior consumers. This sense of community can generate loyalty that transcends whatever momentary pricing or availability advantages your competitors may have. By fostering a sense of community, you can persuade your clients to become your supporters and make frequent returns to your website. This also equips your consumers with the resources they need to suggest your company to an ever-expanding pool of potential prospects.

WHAT IS ADVOCACY MARKETING?

Advocacy marketing is a method of marketing that encourages existing customers of a business to share their experiences with the company and/or its products and/or services, as well as their thoughts about them. This feedback may be publicly accessible in the form of evaluations, utilized by the business itself in marketing materials and content, or simply passed from peer to peer through word of mouth. Regardless of the presentation type, client feedback acts as social evidence for prospective customers. When customers begin promoting or vouching for a firm in any way, they transcend from the role of the customer to that of a brand ambassador. Despite the fact that brand advocates are typically not officially linked with the business, they can be extremely persuasive when expressing their genuine experiences. Since brand advocates are frequently repeat consumers, it is likely that they are knowledgeable about the company's products and services, have firsthand experience with them, and can make informed recommendations to others.

Depending on a business's strategy, the process of producing advocacy marketing may appear differently. However, effective advocacy marketing is based on the building of connections with consumers and clients, as well as the perceived value of doing business with a particular brand. Advocacy marketing is all about encouraging people to speak positively about your brand and products. Meaning that satisfied consumers spread the word about your company via social media or direct word-of-mouth, resulting in the possibility of their network becoming clients as well.

EXAMPLES OF ADVOCACY MARKETING TECHNIQUES UTILIZED BY LEADING BRANDS

Customer experience, as well as brand loyalty, go hand in hand. If you provide clients with an amazing experience, they will spread the word via social media, online reviews, in-person conversations with their friends, and any other means of communication. And customer experience doesn't just mean customer service. It entails embodying and delivering on brand ideals, as well as recognizing and establishing an emotional connection with customers.

Successfully implementing a customer experience plan results in enhanced customer happiness, decreased customer churn, and increased revenue. Often, the recommendations of users can be more powerful than any action taken by the brand alone; hence, businesses are interested in moving and implementing plans to acquire these "brand spokespersons":

1) Airbnb

In 2016, Airbnb topped the YouGov brand advocacy rankings, which examine the number of individuals who refer brands to their friends and family. Airbnb has more brand advocates than any other brand, but how did they accomplish this?

It all boils down to their effective referral campaign. Airbnb users can invite their friends to the platform by sharing an invite link. When they join up and make a reservation, the referrer receives $20 credit, and the referred buddy receives $40 credit. This amount can vary based on location and time. Obviously, $20 off your next reservation is a substantial incentive for users to promote. In addition, having a $20 credit in their account encourages them to book again, ensuring Airbnb repeat business. It's a win-win situation.

Their growth team claims that Airbnb's business model made word-of-mouth referrals from brand advocates especially vital. When individuals are planning to stay in someone's residence, they will have safety concerns. The team believed it was crucial to have someone they knew and trusted who was already a user of Airbnb present to answer questions and advocate for the site. This resulted in the program's spectacular success.

2) Starbucks

Tweet-A-Coffee, a Starbucks advocacy marketing effort, allows people to purchase a $5 Starbucks gift card for a friend via Twitter. Customers just needed to include the Starbucks Tweet-A-Coffee Twitter handle in a tweet with the receiver. The initiative generated $180,000 in purchases, allowing Starbucks to identify prospective customers and devoted supporters.

Inspiring staff advocacy, which in turn drives customer brand advocacy, may be achieved by placing team members first. As a result, Starbucks achieved over 11 percent annual growth in 2017 and a market value of over $84 billion. Brand advocacy not only delights customers but also has a substantial impact on the bottom line growth of a firm.

For most customers, Starbucks represents more than a caffeine break. By fostering a sense of community at its cafés, it has become a "third place" for people in addition to their homes and workplaces. Everything, from the baristas' name games to the music selections, is intended to strengthen the company's relationship with its clients.

3) Naked Wines

Naked Wines is an excellent illustration of an advocate marketing approach. They have an exclusive clientele that they refer to as "Archangels." To promote new wines, assist winemakers, and introduce new users to the website, the company selects its most valuable consumers who have offered word-of-mouth referrals or other forms of value. The company then rewards the Archangels with invitations to exclusive events, sampling of new wines, and participation in a private community where all Naked Wines insider information is revealed first. It appears that the Archangels are quite elite group, as there is a lengthy waiting list. This demonstrates that Naked Wines has a large fan base and is succeeding at something.

4) Apple

The well-known smartphone company utilized UGC as part of its advocate marketing approach. "Shot on iPhone" – Apple's advocacy marketing campaign enabled the company to collect photographs from Apple product users. Customers were encouraged to take photos with their iPhones and post them on social media with a hashtag. Apple selected the best images from the available photos and used them for billboard advertisements. Thus, Apple was able to save on advertising.

5) Nike

Nike is another excellent example of an advocate marketing approach. Nike+ is aware that their clients like healthy competition. Therefore, they created a community that promotes this behavior and emphasizes their other passion... athletics. By hosting challenges, the site maintains advocates' interest (great use of gamification). Customers can then post the outcomes of these challenges on their social networks, creating a direct link to Nike and demonstrating their brand loyalty.

6) Tesla

Recognizing the potential of discounts, Tesla introduced referral packages with substantial discounts for both the existing client and the referred individual. Tesla also incentivizes customers to send more referrals by providing a unique opportunity; for instance, a customer who referred 10 or more individuals to the company was given the opportunity to purchase a limited-edition vehicle that was not available to the general public.

THE SIGNIFICANCE OF ADVOCACY MARKETING

Statistics indicate that 92% of consumers place more weight on personal recommendations than any other form of promotion (Review House, 2021). One of the most efficient ways to sell a product or brand is still word-of-mouth. And this is advantageous for advocacy marketing, as the strategy involves existing customers spreading the word about the product or brand through various media.

This is more effective because these testimonials are from actual clients. Thus, it has a greater effect on those who are considering purchasing the product. As a result of the proliferation of social media, word-of-mouth recommendations now travel further than in the past. The average social media user will have over 400 friends in 2020. That means that each advocate who shares a positive brand experience has the potential to reach 400 individuals.

Simply said, people have faith in their peers' opinions!

Additionally to the well-planned advertising. Thus, advocacy marketing is more effective in increasing sales. The following are some benefits of advocacy marketing:

1) Increase sales

For most businesses, it all comes down to conversions and sales. No software or system is more effective than brand advocates at generating new leads. So the number one reason is sales growth! The budget-friendly and bottom-line-effectiveness of empowering your most ardent supporters with advocacy marketing activities is comparable to that of empowering your most loyal customers. It is the optimal balance between cheap costs and large rewards.

2) Brand champions are respected by their peers

Typically, brand advocates are respected by their peers within their community or network. This does not necessarily imply that a proponent has a huge number of followers. Far more crucial is that the advocate's friends and followers respect his or her viewpoint. Therefore, these peers are interested in trying the brand or product for themselves, and they may also recognize its benefits.

Consider this from the standpoint of an advocate. Perhaps the individual has a website, blog, or social media account that caters to a specific type of person. Or perhaps they simply have a strong network of friends who value their counsel. People that follow an advocate are typical of a similar demographic, share similar interests, or seek the advocate's direction, thoughts, and opinions. The advocate will tell their friends and followers about your product. Then, their peers will be aware of the product and may decide to test it if a credible source has recommended it.

3) Brand advocates are valuable assets

Brand advocates are significant assets since they not only promote your brand but also spend more money and are knowledgeable about your items. This makes them a perfect information source.

4) Advocates will provide reviews

An additional advantage of advocates is that they will gladly provide you with excellent online reviews. The majority of the time, you won't even need to ask since a true advocate will have already done so. We are all aware of the significance of a positive review; therefore, this is excellent news!

5) Revenue growth

The majority of advocacy marketing campaigns (earned, owned, or paid) are centered on referrals — people who will visit you, engage with you, buy from you, and join your team. The more advocates you have, the more options you have to increase your brand's visibility, enhance customer trust, and expand your revenue streams.

ADVOCACY MARKETING STRATEGY

When you exhibit a willingness to meet the demands of your consumers, they will reward you with fervent loyalty. Learn how to generate brand advocacy for your own organization by establishing genuine and enduring emotional ties; when evaluating how to improve a company's advocacy marketing activities, it is crucial to have a well-defined strategy in place. A multifaceted advocacy marketing approach that identifies areas of concentration and basic concepts for producing advocacy marketing activity.

There are five fundamental concepts upon which every effective advocacy marketing campaign is constructed.

1) Determine how you want advocates to interact with potential prospects

Will you have a platform where all of your advocates can interact with you and each other, which will help you create better content? You may just want advocates to act independently. Whatever you decide, you must equip your advocates with the means to advocate. Additionally, you need a method for tracking engagement. This may involve tracking their engagement on a platform or having them email you images of their own engagement.

2) Customer experience

The general enhancement of the business in ways that serve the customers is a crucial element in generating customer advocates. Businesses increase the possibility that customers will recommend a product or service to others or leave an online review by enhancing the customer experience. Before all else, firms should provide the highest quality products and/or services feasible. Without a product that provides value or meets customer expectations, advocacy marketing cannot exist. A business should also discover ways to prioritize the consumer, streamline the sales process as much as possible, and commit to providing exceptional customer service.

. . .

3) Sell a great product or service

Rule number one in the advocacy marketing manual is to ensure that your customers have a reason to promote your products or services. It makes no significant difference how much effort you put into marketing or the quality of your customer service. If you do not provide a superior product or service, they will not become brand ambassadors.

On the other side, a superior product or service can compensate for poor marketing and a negative consumer experience overall.

4) Tactical strategies

There is a selection of ways in which a firm can increase the participation of advocates to promote its marketing activities. Creating opportunities for their devoted customers to advocate for the company is a primary method for achieving this goal. This may involve following up with customers for product reviews after they have received or purchased a product, creating in-store attractions and environments that beg to be photographed and shared on social media, or simply creating digital content that addresses customer questions or is inherently shareable. All of these strategies are designed to allow customers to express their affection, voice, or opinion regarding the business.

5) Search for supporters

Customers who are really satisfied with your products or services are the ideal brand ambassadors. But you cannot organize them if you are unaware of their identities. Therefore, you must also make an effort to locate them. When you launch your advocacy marketing campaign, you will be able to better personalize your marketing communications and personally contact these satisfied customers once you have identified them.

AFTERWORD

Customer service is the backbone of any organization. The company that spends the most time communicating with their customers, comprehending their wants, resolving their problems, and providing their voice.

Each connection is integral to a longer customer journey that builds trust and fosters long-term relationships. Without excellent customer service, we would likely lose customers quickly. If done correctly, customer service can also generate one of the greatest revenue opportunities: referrals from satisfied customers. Whether your company is brand new or has been providing customer care for years, it never hurts to review the fundamentals of customer service.

Customer service abilities are essential to your company's success. Even more than price, a pleasant customer experience may differentiate a business from its competition. Businesses that recognize this advantage frequently go to great lengths to enhance the customer experience. They expand their support channels, customize their products, and make decisions that are more customer-centric.

Help others acquire this knowledge and expertise by writing a convincing **Amazon review.**

DISCUSSION SECTION

Here are a few things worth mentioning:

- Customer dissatisfaction arises when the actual customer service engagement falls short of the customer's expectations. Almost three-quarters of consumers anticipate that you will comprehend their demands and expectations (**Meena Toor, 2020**).

- Customers want businesses to connect with them by their preferred method, be it in-person, online, or via phone. Depending on the type of inquiry, modern consumers want to be able to contact you via at least 10 distinct channels.

- Consumers have more options than ever before. Due to the continuously rising variety of options, it is difficult to rectify negative encounters. Once upon a time, businesses were able to get away with subpar customer service because consumers lacked alternatives. They had to go back. Today, the tide has shifted, and there are a great number of competitors. A simple Google search is sufficient to find a new supplier. People are discouraged when they seek your goods online and encounter an unresolved negative review. According to a study, it takes twelve favorable evaluations to change a potential customer's mind (**Daniel Newman, 2015**).

- What is your customer service like? Recent research indicates that customers will spend 31% more with organizations that have received outstanding evaluations (**Rebekah Carter, 2022**). This should explain the recent behavior of your customers. The amount of business you receive, particularly repeat business, reflects the effectiveness of your customer service.

- Customer service week is observed annually during the first week of October. It is a time when businesses express gratitude to their staff and consumers for their support and patronage. You can also utilize this time to make changes to your customer service policies.

- Customers are no longer loyal based on pricing or product. Instead, individuals remain loyal to companies because of their experiences with them. Customers will abandon you if you are unable to meet their ever-increasing demands.

- 57% of clients will not suggest a company with a badly designed mobile website (**Sweor, 2022**). And fifty percent of clients will quit visiting a website if it is not mobile-friendly, even if they like the firm. If you fail to offer a pleasant mobile experience, you endanger your business's success.

SOURCES

Abella, A. (2017 April, 7th). 6 Reasons why business owners should focus on follow-ups. *Due.* **https://due.com/blog/follow-ups/amp/**

Bansal, T. & Agarwal, D. (2021 March, 10th). Corporate sustainability: Meaning, example and importance. *Network for business sustainability.* **https://nbs. net/articles/corporate-sustainability-meaning-examples-and-impor tance/**

Basin. K. (2011). 15 facts about coca-cola that will blow your mind: 94% of the world's population recognises their logo for awareness. *Businessinsider.* **https://www.google.com/amp/s/www.businessinsider.com/facts-about-coca-cola-2011-6%3famp**

Bright ideas. (2022) . Local Consumer Review Survey 2022. *BrightLocal.* **https:// www.brightlocal.com/research/local-consumer-review-survey/**

Brzezicki, A. (2021 October, 7th). Brand loyalty: Why it matters, how to get it, and how to measure it. *Bazaarvoive blog.* **https://www.bazaarvoice.com/ blog/brand-loyalty-why-it-matters-and-how-to-measure-it/**

Daniel Newman, N. (2015 October, 13th). Customer experience is the future of marketing. *Forbes.* **https://www.forbes.com/sites/danielnewman/2015/ 10/13/customer-experience-is-the-future-of-marketing/?sh= 69018ab8193d**

Deane. T. M. & Beer. K. (2022). Top 6 reasons business fail. *Investopedia.* **https:// www.investopedia.com/financial-edge/1010/top-6-reasons-new-busi nesses-fail.aspx**

Dinardi, G. (2019, June, 14). 15 Customer service psychology tips to master. let's go! *Nextiva.* **https://www.nextiva.com/blog/customer-service-psycholo gy.html**

Dorronsoro, S. (2022 July, 1st). What is brand loyalty and how can companies build it. *Brandwatch.* **https://www.brandwatch.com/blog/brand-loyalty/**

F. Dennis. (2018). Omnichannel CX: How to overcome technology's artificial divide and succeed at being seamless. *Forbes.* **https://www.forbes.com/ sites/forbestechcouncil/2018/06/15/omnichannel-cx-how-to-over come-technologys-artificial-divide-and-succeed-at-being-seamless/**

Green, E. (2019 June, 4th). The what, why, and how of a brand promise. *Olive& & Co.* **https://www.oliveandcompany.com/blog/the-what-why-and-how-of-a-brand-promise**

Indeed Editorial Team. (2021 June, 24th). Understanding Advocacy Marketing:

Definition, Benefits and Tips. *Indeed.* https://www.indeed.com/career-advice/career-development/advocacy-marketing

Innovation Visual Ltd. Everything you need to know about paid advertising. https://www.innovationvisual.com/knowledge/everything-you-need-to-know-about-paid-advertising

Kemp. S. (2020). Digital 2020: Global digital overview. *DataReportal.* https://datareportal.com/reports/digital-2020-global-digital-overview

Kopp, M, C & Mansa, J. (2021 June, 30th). *Brand Loyalty.* Investopedia.https://www.investopedia.com/terms/b/brand-loyalty.asp

Laja, P. (2019 April, 2019). Purchase Decisions: 9 things to know about influencing customers. *CXL.* https://cxl.com/blog/9-things-to-know-about-influencing-purchasing-decisions/amp/

Las, D, S. (2019 September, 2019). Why keeping your Brand Promise matters to your business. *Medium.* https://medium.com/swlh/why-keeping-your-brand-promise-matters-to-your-business-d18164a998fd.

Meena Toor, M. (2020 December, 3rd). Customer expectations: 7 Types all exceptional researchers must understand. *Qualtrics.* https://www.qualtrics.com/blog/customer-expectations/

Nextiva Blog. (2021). 100 Essential Customer Service Statistics and Trends for 2022. https://www.nextiva.com/blog/customer-service-statistics.html

Ouellette, C. (2022 January, 2022). Online shopping statistics you need to know in 2022. *Optinmonster.* https://optinmonster.com/online-shopping-statistics/

Rebekah Carter, R. (2022 April, 9th). The ultimate list of online review statistics for 2022. *Findstack.* https://findstack.com/online-review-statistics/

Review House. (2021 January, 28th). 92% of consumers trust word of mouth. *Buyapowa.* https://www.buyapowa.com/blog/92-of-consumers-trust-word-of-mouth/

Schmaltz, H. (2021 September, 2nd). Why innovation is essential for business success. *Masterclass.* https://www.masterclass.com/articles/why-innovation-is-essential-for-business-success#quiz-0

Schwantes, M.(2022 April, 5th). *Inc.Africa.* 3 in 5 employees would consider quitting because of this reason, research says. https://incafrica.com/article/marcel-schwantes-3-in-5-employees-would-consider-quitting-because-of-this-reason-research-says

Schwartz. E.M. (2004). Breakthrough advertising. **My Book**

Smith. M. (2022). 111 Customer Service Statistics and facts you shouldn't ignore. *Help scout.* https://www.helpscout.com/75-customer-service-facts-quotes-statistics/

Sweor. (2022 January, 20th). 27 Eye-Opening Website Statistics: Is your website costing you clients? https://www.sweor.com/firstimpressions

Talal Rafi, T. (2021 February, 10th). Why corporate Strategies should be focused on sustainability. *Forbes.* **https://www.forbes.com/sites/deloitte/2022/ 05/16/the-new-sustainability-paradigm-for-tech-making-measure ment-more-meaningful/?sh=1241aab3648d**

Theodore Henderson, T. (2017 May, 8th). Why innovation is crucial to your organization's long-term success. *Forbes.* **https://www.forbes.com/sites/ forbescoachescouncil/2017/05/08/why-innovation-is-crucial-to-your- organizations-long-term-success/?sh=32986f603098**

Townsend, C. (2019 December, 2019). *The good alliance.* Why consistency is the key to business success. **https://thegoodalliance.org/articles/consis tency-key-to-business-success/**

Waksman, K. (2020 January, 2nd). How to choose the eight distribution channel for your business. **https://www.thebalancesmb.com/choose- best-distribution-channel-for-your-business-3502272**

West, C. (2021). 100+ branding statistics you need to know in 2022. *Visme.* **https://visme.co/blog/branding-statistics/**

Zaltman. G. (2020). *Ignite sales.* 95% of purchasing decisions are emotional – what that means for FIs. How Customers Think: Essential Insights into the Mind of the Market. **https://ignitesales.com/blog/95-of-purchasing-deci sions-are-emotional/**